I0466650

Forex Rules

WHAT TO DO AND WHAT NOT TO DO, IN
ORDER TO SUCCEED

Andres E. Pedraza

The Lemic Group, Inc.
NESQUEHONING, PENNSYLVANIA

Copyright © 2024 by Andres E. Pedraza.

All rights reserved. No part of this publication may be reproduced, distributed, or transmitted in any form or by any means, including photocopying, recording, or other electronic or mechanical methods, without the prior written permission of the publisher, except in the case of brief quotations embodied in critical reviews and certain other noncommercial uses permitted by copyright law. For permission requests, write to the publisher, addressed "Attention: Permissions Coordinator," at the address below.

AEP/The Lemic Group, Inc.
2 East Catawissa St
Nesquehoning, PA 18240
www.thelemicgroup.com

Book Layout ©2013 BookDesignTemplates.com

Ordering Information:
Quantity sales. Special discounts are available on quantity purchases by corporations, associations, and others. For details, contact the "Special Sales Department" at the address above.

Forex Rules/Andres E. Pedraza —1st ed.

Table of Contents

Preface 13

Rule #1 19

    You Cannot Predict the Market 19

    What to Do Instead 21

Rule #2 23

    You Cannot Win Them All 23

    What to Do Instead 26

Rule #3 28

    Don't Marry Your Losing Trades 28

    What to Do Instead 30

Rule #4 32

    Don't Take Profit Too Soon 32

    What to Do Instead 33

Rule #5 34

    Don't Have Unreasonable Expectations 34

    What to Do Instead 37

Rule #6 39

   Control Risk, the Rest Will Control Itself (Trade and Single Account Risk) 39

      What to Do 41

Rule #7 43

   Nobody is Handing Out Free Money.......................43

      What to Do Instead 47

Rule #8 48

   The Market isn't Going Anywhere 48

      What to Do 49

Rule #9 51

   You Don't Need to Win 51% of the Time or More in Order to be Successful 51

      What to Do Instead 53

Rule #10 55

   Long Term Outperforms Short Term 55

      What to Do 57

Rule #11 58

   You Will Not Get Rich Overnight..............................58

    What to Do Instead 62

Rule #12 63

    Compounding is Your Best Friend 63

    What to Do 67

Rule #13 68

    Trends Are Your Other Best Friend 68

    What to Do 70

Rule #14 71

    Trading is Boring, Except When it Isn't 71

    What to Do 73

Rule #15 74

    You Can't Have Quotas 74

    What to Do Instead 77

Rule #16 79

    Trade Broadly, Trade Often 79

    What to Do 80

Rule #17 82

    Don't Overtrade 82

  What to Do Instead 85

Rule #18 87

  Trade with a System, Always 87

  What to Do 89

Rule #19 92

  Don't Reinvent the Wheel 92

  What to Do Instead 94

Rule #20 96

  Don't Pay for Stuff that's Free or Unnecessary 96

  What to Do Instead 96

Rule #21 100

  Slow and Steady Wins the Race 100

  What to Do 101

Rule #22 104

  Leverage is Necessary 104

  What to Do 107

Afterword 108

Appendix I 109

  Systems for Trading 110

Turtle Trading	113
3-Screen System	116
One Last Thing	121
ABOUT THE AUTHOR	125

Dedicated to my mentors, too many to list.

When ancient opinions and rules of life are taken away, the loss cannot possibly be estimated. From that moment, we have no compass to govern us, nor can we know distinctly to what port to steer.

—Edmund Burke, Anglo-Irish statesman and philosopher

DISCLAIMER

Trading in the financial markets carries a high level of risk and may not be suitable for everyone. When applicable, the high degree of leverage can work against you as well as in your favor. Before deciding to trade you should carefully consider your investment objectives, level of experience, and tolerance for risk. The possibility exists that you could sustain a loss of some, all, or even more than your initial capital and/or account balance at any given time, and therefore you should not trade with money that you cannot afford to lose. You should be aware of all the risks associated with trading and seek advice from an independent financial advisor if you have any questions.

Any statements regarding income, whether expressed or implied, do NOT represent a guarantee. No representation is being made that any trading account will or is likely to achieve profits or losses like those shown. Any opinions, news, research, analysis, prices, or other information contained in this book are provided as general market commentary, for educational purposes only, and do not constitute investment advice nor a solicitation to buy or sell any forex contract or securities of any type. The author and publishers will not accept liability for any loss or damage, including without limitation any loss of profit and/or equity, which may arise directly or indirectly from use of or reliance on the information contained in this book or associated material published by us elsewhere.

ANY RESULTS PROVIDED ARE BASED ON SIMULATED OR HYPOTHETICAL PERFORMANCE RESULTS THAT HAVE CERTAIN INHERENT LIMITATIONS. UNLIKE THE RESULTS SHOWN IN AN ACTUAL PERFORMANCE RECORD, THESE RESULTS DO NOT REPRESENT ACTUAL TRADING. ALSO, BECAUSE THESE TRADES HAVE NOT ACTUALLY BEEN EXECUTED, THESE RESULTS MAY HAVE UNDER-OR OVER-COMPENSATED FOR THE IMPACT, IF ANY, OF CERTAIN MARKET FACTORS, SUCH AS LACK OF LIQUIDITY. SIMULATED OR HYPOTHETICAL TRADING SYSTEMS OR STRATEGIES IN GENERAL ARE ALSO SUBJECT TO THE FACT THAT THEY ARE DESIGNED WITH THE BENEFIT OF HINDSIGHT. NO REPRESENTATION IS BEING MADE THAT ANY ACCOUNT WILL OR IS LIKELY TO ACHIEVE PROFITS OR LOSSES SIMILAR TO THOSE BEING SHOWN.

The information as presented is based solely on the author's experience and acquired knowledge. Please note that simulated trading results may or may not have been back tested for accuracy and that spreads/commissions are not considered when preparing hypothetical results. Pips captured represent net or overall pips for the trading period indicated.

Preface

Fifteen years ago, I started trading the Forex Market with as much seriousness as I dedicated to my former day job and treating it as a business instead of a hobby. Before that, for maybe 3 or so years, I'd treated it as an occasional pursuit, one that made me money with some *ir*regularity. And there's nothing wrong with that, nor with you doing it that way. Some people spend lots of money collecting stamps. That's called a hobby. I collected some money by trading forex occasionally. That was also a hobby. It definitely wasn't a business. It didn't produce consistent returns. I couldn't budget around it.

It. Was. A. Hobby.

Sixteen years ago (2008) something disrupted my world. If you think it was the global financial crisis, give yourself a pat on the back. My six-figure salary job went away. I was let go, along with thousands of other people, and that was just one company. I didn't even bother looking for a job. I was totally burned out. I went back to school to study to be a paramedic. That's a pretty short study track. It's less than a year, and you get to save people's lives, run red lights, get coffee at Wawa[1] at 3 in the morning, pump drugs into people

---

[1] A regional 24-hour convenience store with decent

having the worst day of their lives, flirt with hot nurses, and other fun stuff. Compared to my job as an IT Service Manager for highly demanding customers, it was zero stress. After all, it wasn't me having the worst day of my life, it was someone else. And once I handed them off to the pretty nurse at the hospital, or the way-too-serious-for-his-own-good doctor, I'd never see them again. No work to take home. No emergency meetings on my days off. Bliss.

Unfortunately, no six-figure salary, either. Now, I'd been trading stocks since the early nineties. I'd been trading options since the early noughties. I'd made money with both, but always as an occasional thing. I'd have this great idea that an unknown company called Amazon that sold books online was going to be a big thing one day, and I'd buy a thousand shares at $4. I'd think there's no way that Apple is going to disappear, and buy a thousand shares of them, coincidentally, also at $4. Later I'd do the same with options contracts instead of outright buying shares because of the greater leverage. Had I done that at the time with Amazon, Apple, and all the others, I wouldn't have bothered with a thousand shares, I would have controlled ten thousand shares of each, and probably with less money down.

But I only had those ideas occasionally. I didn't have the time to really study the market and a thousand companies all the time and have my ideas every day or every week. So, I'd parlay one of my ideas into a few tens of thousands of

coffee.

dollars every year or so, which nicely supplemented my salary. But I always lived off my salary. The trading profit was like a bonus. It kept me in good whiskey (Laphroaig, if you must know, and not the ten-year one) and other nice things in life.

However, I'd discovered the Forex Market around 2005-ish. Its technical analysis was the same as with stocks, so there was nothing new to learn. *A chart is a chart is a chart*, is how I usually explain it to traders unfamiliar with Forex. The fundamentals are way easier to analyze than with a company. There are no balance sheets, SEC filings, competitor analysis, shareholder meetings, or the like to track. Sure, the financials of the US Dollar are the entire US economy, but that's macroeconomics. It might sound daunting compared to a company's filings, but I assure you, it's the opposite.

Also, there are only 8 major currencies, as opposed to the tens of thousands, if not more, companies listed in the major stock markets. Learn 8 currencies well, and you can trade them against each other all the time, except weekends. That's another advantage. The Forex Market runs non-stop, without closing, 24 hours a day, 5 days a week. Plus, you don't even need to specialize in all 8 currencies. Learn only one or two well, and I assure you that you can make profits consistently.

But here's the key thing. If you want consistency, it can't be a hobby. It must be a business, it can't be something you do when you're bored, or when you want to relax from the day job. It must be something you operate formally, with you as the CEO. With operating guidelines. With working hours set in advance. With working capital. With rules.

Losing my job in 2008, through no fault of my own, was a wake-up call. I promised myself never ever again to be in that situation. To never again allow someone else to control my livelihood. Never to make millions for a company and be happy they allowed me to keep $100,000 a year for myself ($100,000 was my salary when I was let go in 2008). I did get a nice severance package, though. That allowed me to plan my career switch to paramedic and, more importantly, also have a decent amount of working capital to move from hobby trading into trading like a business.

Along the way, I discovered the rules that I needed to implement to succeed. Over the years, I've helped others to succeed in trading, which led me to discover other rules that needed to be applied. Many of them I already had. Call them my unwritten rules. But I discovered that others didn't have them, and so they needed to be written down. This book is that, it's the rules written down. You may already know some of them. Hopefully, you do. If you're completely new to trading, then they might all be new to you. That's alright, too.

What this book isn't is a guide on how to trade. I already wrote that book[2]. I even hinted at some of these rules in it, but I hadn't taught Forex yet, at the time. Most of these rules were fleshed out by seeing where my students were having problems. Sometimes by seeing where prospects who never let themselves be taught by me were having problems. Everything that should be a rule became a rule. If anything, this book is primarily a How-Not-To book. Avoid the issues I point out, and you'll be well on your way to lasting success. As Warren Buffett of Berkshire Hathaway is often quoted as saying, *"The first rule of an investment is don't lose [money]. And the second rule of an investment is don't forget the first rule. And that's all the rules there are."* This applies just as well to trading. While I agree with Warren, you should take that quote with a grain of salt. He was being humorous. Warren **has** lost money. But his approach is such that his winners vastly outperform his losers, so that overall, he **does not** lose money.

My rules are designed to help you "not lose money", but they're useful and specific, even if lacking in Warren's folksiness. Follow all of them, and you'll also be following Warren's rules #1 and #2.

Between my actual How-To book, and this How-Not-To addition, you should be squared away for the best possible outcome, **if** you follow what I've written to the letter. That's not to say that you can never stray from what I've written. What it means is that you should start operating the way I'm

---

[2] http://amzn.to/3ANrLF5

telling you to. Only with experience will you know when and how to break the rules. And even then, some rules cannot be broken with impunity, because they are as immutable as physical laws.

This book, then, is all the things to do and not to do. I can categorically state that, if you follow them, you will have a very hard time not making money. Respect yourself, respect the market, and respect trading. It will then respect you back.

BOOK ONE – THE KEY RULES

Rule #1

You Cannot Predict the Market

This is the absolute, most important, most critical rule. No one, not me, not Warren Buffett, not Ray Dalio, not the talking head on Bloomberg TV, and certainly, not you, can ever predict what the market is going to do. Yet almost everyone who starts trading seems to be under the impression that a) successful traders can and do predict the market and b) they need to learn this magic skill.

In marketing there's a saying, *"give the customers what they want"*. The commonly held belief that the market is predictable has spawned a cottage industry of shysters and scammers offering to teach market prediction techniques and/or sell *bogus systems* that pretend to do this for you automatically. The amount of money collectively spent in the pursuit of crystal ball systems could probably power a decently sized hedge fund, and individually I've seen people mortgage and lose their homes in this foolish and unnecessary quest.

Markets aren't rational. The irrational can never be predicted. Markets are mob psychology in the purest sense. Would you ever pay the price of a house for a tulip bulb? Normally, no. But get caught in mob behavior and you most definitely would. Some otherwise very rational people did just that, during the Tulipmania Craze in Holland. Tulips were worth more than gold for a brief period, and just as suddenly became worthless, wiping out both new and old fortunes. Bitcoin enthusiasts, take note.

> A single bulb could be worth as much as 4,000 or even 5,500 florins. Because 1630s florins were gold coins of uncertain weight and quality, it is hard to make an accurate estimation of today's value in dollars, but Scottish journalist Charles Mackay, in his famous 1841 book Memoirs of Extraordinary Popular Delusions and the Madness of Crowds[3], does give us some points of reference: Among other things, 4 tuns of beer cost 32 florins. That's around 1,008 gallons of beer, or 65 kegs of beer. A keg of Coors Light costs around $120, so 4 tuns of beer ≈ $7,800 and 1 florin ≈ $244.23 This means that the best of tulips cost upwards of $1 million in today's money (but with many bulbs trading in the $50,000–$150,000 range). By 1636, the demand for the tulip trade was so large that regular marts for their sale were established on the Stock Exchange of Amsterdam, in Rotterdam, Haarlem, and other towns.[4]

---

[3] https://amzn.to/3SNmoyt

[4] https://www.investopedia.com/terms/d/dutch_tulip_bulb_market_bubble.asp

While markets don't always act that crazily, they still act with disconcerting unpredictability all the time. And that means that you will never, ever be able to predict the market, so don't even try. And, if you've been trying, please stop.

What to Do Instead

Do not try to predict. Money is made in the markets by trading with the market, not by trying to anticipate it. That means that you'll have to wait for the market to move, and then trade in its direction. While it would be fantastic to buy at the absolute low and get out at the absolute high, that's not possible. In any market move that you successfully trade, you will miss the initial 10% to 20% of the move, since that will be the trigger for your entry signal, coming in **after** the move has already begun. You will then enter the trade and capture the middle portion of the move. The final 10% to 20% will also be missed, because you don't know where it will stop. You will either exit too early and watch it move even further in what would have been your favor or get out too late after it has retraced somewhat against you. The good news is that this still means you're capturing between 60% to 80% of the movement. That's more than enough if you're consistently finding such trades.

Along the way, you're also going to be entered into trades that don't work out and will lose small amounts in these. Your winners should make up for these, and still leave net profit.

The way you do the above is by having a trading system that identifies opportunities (after that initial move) and keeps you in the winning trades for as long as possible, before getting you out on a retrace or whatever other exit criteria your system has. Having a system, or more than one, is key. You cannot succeed without a system and the discipline to follow it. More on systems later. Discretionary traders either have a system, even if they don't admit to it, or have very short careers.

Rule #2

You Cannot Win Them All

Hand in hand with the idea that you can predict the market, comes the idea that every trade needs to be a winner. Even I suffered from this one. Well, not consciously since I already knew Rule #1. Obviously, if you cannot predict the market, it stands to reason that not every trade will be a winner. You are going to have losing trades and losing periods. Nonetheless, I noticed I'd feel actual shame if someone saw my account while I had open trades that were carrying a loss, or worse, if they noticed my account was down from where it was the last time they'd seen it. This became more obvious when I started trading publicly and posting monthly results.

And the thing is, you cannot close a losing trade the minute it starts going against you. In fact, all trades start against you, simply because of the spread[5]. We assign each trade a stop loss, that's plain common sense, but it's still a bit daunting to check your trades and find a sea of red, with

---

[5] The difference between the Ask and Bid quotes, which is typically what the broker makes on each customer trade, upfront, as soon as you open it.

all or most moving against you, but not at your stop losses yet. It's even worse if someone's looking at your account. I keenly felt that. I knew Rule #1, and I also knew Rule #2, but I still felt it!

Eventually, I got over it. Nowadays, I can be down overall, and not blink an eye. If someone asks me, I'll happily show them. It is perfectly normal to have losing trades open. Funny thing, many a time those losers come back and become winners. Since we cannot predict the market, it stands to reason that even when we find a good entry, it can move against us initially. I have lost count of how many times I've been carrying a 100-pip losing trade that, a week or three, later becomes a 500-pip winner.

Of course, sometimes those open trades carrying a loss continue on to hit their stop loss and do take me out at a loss. This, too, is normal. Cost of doing business. Eventually, if you're doing things right, you'll hit your stride. You'll find out that out of every 10 trades you open, 4 will hit their stop loss, 4 will go on to do not much of anything (winning or losing a little), and 2 will go on to sky-high profits. These last cover the losers and then some. But here's the thing, Rule #1 again, when you open the 10 trades, you have no idea which is which. The 4 losers are the cost of doing business. They are the price you pay to expose yourself to the 2 big winners. No losing trades, no big winners. The only way to avoid those losers is not to trade at all!

Now, your win/loss distribution may be different. Over time, you may find that for every 10 trades that you open, you'll have 3 losers, 6 flat trades, and 1 winner. It doesn't matter as long as the combined net profit is positive. If every time you open 10 trades the result is a 2% gain in your account, who cares how many are losers? It's the same with any other business. Who cares if they spend $100,000 each month between rent, loan servicing, payroll, taxes, supplies, utilities, merchandise, advertising, and other expenses, if they have monthly revenue totaling $180,000? They net a profit of $80,000 each month. Guess what happens if they decide it's a bad idea to spend the $100,000?

There is no business out there that has only income and no expenses. None. Trading is no different. The spreads or commissions you pay, your Internet connection, your losing trades, they are the equivalent of the rent, payroll, supplies, utilities, and whatnot that a brick and mortar business owner pay out. There is no shame in that. Imagine if a gas station owner felt any shame when writing out the rent checks or paying the employees. Silly, right?

That needs to be us. I am not saying you should fall in love with your losers, but you should have a little warm spot for them. They're the price you pay for your winnings. All that, of course, if you do have net profits at the end of every 10 trades, or 50, or whatever number you're measuring against, overall. Your account needs to be growing over time, but not necessarily every day, nor every week, nor every month. Losing trades and losing periods are perfectly normal as long as they're not sustained and ever-increasing losses.

If you are consistently losing, over longer periods of time, that's a problem you need to address. Your *system*, whichever one you're using to select trades, isn't working. That doesn't invalidate what I said above, but it does mean you have to hit the pause button and reevaluate what you're doing. We will cover that later in this book.

What to Do Instead

Accept that losing trades are inevitable. Make sure that they're always small losses, measured as a percentage of your total funds. Learn how to measure risk down to the penny and have strict limits on how much risk per trade is permitted. Trades that exceed that risk, even if legitimately signaled by your trade entry system should be rejected or, alternatively, taken at a smaller position size to reduce the risk to where it falls within your parameters. Since any trade can lose, some will. Never allow a trade to lose more than you can afford to lose in one trade.

Also, make sure you have a maximum overall percentage of loss that triggers a trading halt and a reassessment. If your system isn't working, don't just keep at it. That's insane. I have a 30% maximum drawdown rule. If my account is 30%

off its high, I stop and figure out what's going wrong. You don't have to use 30%. Yours can be higher or lower. But it should never be so much that recovery becomes too difficult or even impossible. As in, if you lost 90% of your account, you're not going to do much with the remaining 10%. You'd need a 1,000% gain just to bring it back up to where you were before. Never allow matters to get that far out of hand.

Rule #3

Don't Marry Your Losing Trades

When we have what we think is a good entry for a trade (based on the *system* we're using), we go in. And we should immediately set a reasonable stop loss. The stop loss is determined by whatever system we're using to select trades, it can't be arbitrary. Not to get into it too much, as I cover this in other books, but it could be a multiple of the ATR (Average True Range) for the chart, it could be a specific number of pips above or below the most recent significant high or low, or something altogether different but indicated by the system you're using.

There is always the temptation to move the stop loss further away if the trade is going against you and approaching the stop loss, especially if you firmly believe in the trade. You think that it might be on the verge of turning around in your favor, if only you give it a bit more wiggle room. And, believe me, that does happen sometimes. The trade hits your stop loss, takes you out, and then that pair turns around and moves far, far in your expected direction. But you're no longer in it. It's not a fun feeling.

Don't. Don't ever fall for that temptation. Don't get married or otherwise emotionally attached to a losing trade. While you may get away with it here and there, far more often what will happen is that the trade continues moving against you, racking up losses well beyond what you would have originally lost if you'd left the stop loss alone. I never move a stop loss further away, for any reason. If I move a stop loss, it will be moved in my favor, to protect profit as it accrues, never against me.

I've seen traders wipe out accounts because they couldn't let go of losing trades, always waiting for the market to prove they were right. Don't worry about being wrong, worry about not losing too much, and worry about making a net profit every so many trades. Every dollar you lose above what you originally intended to lose if you were wrong, is a dollar being taken out of your overall net profit. Do that too many times, and that's how net profits turn into net losses. I'm thrilled being wrong more than half of the time if my account doubles in size every year.

There's a saying in trading circles, *cut your losses short and let your winners run*. I don't agree with it. I prefer, **cut your losses where you said you would and let your winners run**. You already expected x number of losers. Let it happen. But only allow them to lose the original amount your system told you to risk. Getting out too soon is also bad,[6] because some of those losers will turn around before hitting your stop loss, but you don't know which ones. Some of those could even become any of your few big winners. Trust your system unless it clearly isn't working.

What to Do Instead

Have a *trading system* exclusive to each trading account you operate.[7] A trading system is the bedrock of your trading. Your trading system will tell you when to enter a trade, how much to risk on it, and when to exit it. It takes all the guesswork out of trading and keeps temptation at bay. The trading system will set the stop loss and tell you how to adjust it on trades moving in your favor. On the losers, and there will be losers, you will get taken out at the stop loss, or even earlier, if the system indicates you should exit a trade before it even hits its stop. You cannot avoid having losers, but you can limit the amount of your losses. And you can

---

[6] Except when the underlying circumstances, and hence, reasons for being in the trade, change.

[7] The reason for exclusivity by account is because trading systems operate with different criteria and on different timeframes. If you use more than one trading system on a single account, you run the risk of getting simultaneous and conflicting trade entries, such as going long and short at the same time on the same pair. There is nothing wrong with using more than one system, just do so on separate accounts, or on a single account, but at different times.

only do that if you're following a system. Otherwise, you will fall into the temptation to give losers just a little bit more room, in the hope that they'll turn around. That's not how it works. If you do that, your only result will be losing trades that lose more than you can afford. We will, of course, be coming back to trading systems further on in this book.

Rule #4

Don't Take Profit Too Soon

This problem is often found in combination with not following the previous rule. Some traders do get attached to losing trades and let them lose far more than they'd planned. So, when a winner comes along, they want to close it out as soon as it's showing green. This allows them to put that trade in the win column. It makes them feel better, psychologically speaking, but not their account. Their account, if it had feelings, would be nauseous.

It should be obvious what the results will be. Using my stats as an example, if I didn't follow Rules #3 and #4, I'd end up with 4 big losers (because I moved the stop loss), 4 flat trades, and 2 tiny winners (because I closed them out early). The winning trades would have no chance of covering for the losing trades because I didn't let them win enough.

Whatever system you are following has 3 key components. It will identify entries, determine the initial stop loss, and determine how and when to take profit. It must be followed to the letter! When to take profit may involve setting a limit when the trade is open, setting a trailing stop, or some alternate method. There is almost never a valid reason to exit a winning trade before the system has indicated an exit.[8]

I have never seen violations of rules #1 through #4 end in anything less than disaster. This is why I placed them in front of all the others.

What to Do Instead

Have a *trading system* exclusive to each trading account you operate. A trading system is the bedrock of your trading. Your trading system will tell you when to enter a trade, how much to risk on it, and when to exit it. It takes all the guesswork out of trading and keeps temptation at bay. The trading system will set the limit (take profit) and/or adjust the stop on trades moving in your favor. This will maximize your profits on your larger winners, as well as exit you with some profit on many smaller movers along the way. We will,

---

[8] The one exception is if something has materially changed that would affect the premise behind the trade. For example, I am trading on Yen strength and there's just been a Major Tsunami Warning issued for Japan. I not only want to close my Yen strength trades, but I also probably want to open some Yen weakness trades if the market hasn't reacted yet.

as already mentioned, be coming back to trading systems further on in this book.

Rule #5

Don't Have Unreasonable Expectations

I interview every single trader and prospective trader before I let them buy any of my products, apart from my books. Everyone else has at least one interview before I even allow them to enroll or subscribe. It's more for my protection than theirs.

There's an episode of Friends where Monica's then boyfriend, a very wealthy individual, suddenly decided he wanted to be the World Champion of Cage Fighting, or something similar. It was sort of a caricature of Elon Musk well before Elon Musk was a household name. Uncannily prophetic, but I digress. This was not a young man in peak condition, this was a man pushing thirty, maybe even on the wrong side of thirty. He would be competing with fighters training since childhood, and they would be in peak condition, as well as younger. He hired a trainer. That trainer should have immediately rejected him, no matter how much money was dangled. The expectations were impossibly unrealistic.

The result was predictable. The boyfriend ended up in a full body cast.

When I started teaching, I firmly believed that I could train anybody to be a successful trader. I was soon disabused of that notion. One of the main reasons why I can't turn everyone into successful traders is expectations. I am not going to publish my interview questions, but I will mention a few throughout this book, and a very important one is:

How much do you expect/need to make by trading? What amount of money per year would spell success for you?

That's one question, it's just phrased two different ways. It is paired with another one:

How much trading capital do you have available?

Those who say they have less than US$1,000 and want to make US$100,000 or more every year make up most applicants. It's not totally their fault. I've seen the ads for trading coaches. They imply, if not outright state, that you can double your money every week. That they'll teach you how to never lose. They show photoshopped account statements with hundreds of thousands of dollars in profit per month. People unfamiliar with trading are bombarded by these ads as soon as they do a Google search on trading. Try it out. You'll see what I mean.

Here's the reality. The S&P 500 has grown 10.13% averaged annually since its inception in 1957. Those are very decent returns, especially thanks to compounding. Note that this annualized average growth includes periods of market retracement. It's still a brilliant record of growth, and a testament to capitalism and the free market. Berkshire Hathaway all but doubles that, even more impressively, coming in at a 19.8% annualized return since 1965, when it started. It, too, has had negative years.

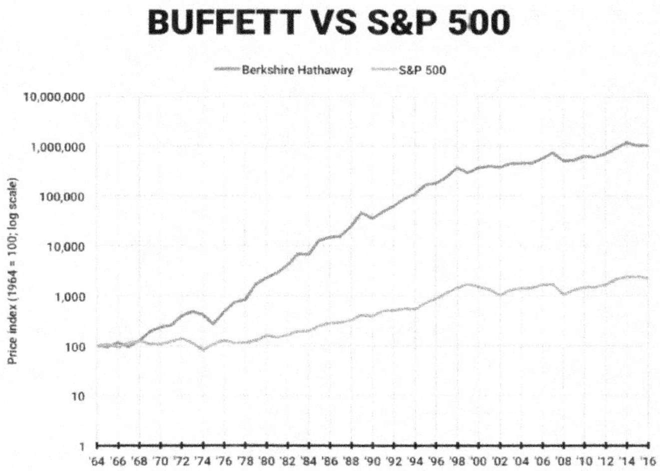

BUFFETT VS S&P 500

Figure 1 - Comparing Berkshire Hathaway's Performance Against the S&P 500

Now, these are professionals operating for over 60 odd years, and considered the best of the best, combining excellent returns without taking extraordinary risks. If you want to beat those returns, besides impeccable skill, you will have to take much bigger risks. I personally clock in at around 75% annualized average returns over the last 10-year period,[9] and I'll readily admit that I've had bigger drawdowns than Warren Buffett (Berkshire Hathaway's founder and CEO) along the way. That's to be expected.

Back to expectations. You cannot expect to make a hundred thousand in a year from a thousand dollar account. You can, if you are extremely good at it, perhaps double your money every year. That means that after a year of trading, your thousand dollars have become two thousand dollars. That is superb, coming in at ten times the S&P 500, and five times Berkshire Hathaway, but it's still two thousand dollars. Yes, it does take money to make money.

What to Do Instead

Your expectations need to be reasonable. Of course, if you double your money every year and don't otherwise

---

[9] Why am I not richer than Buffett? Easy. I've been at it for a much shorter period and with a lot less capital. I will never catch up to Warren, and I'm fine with that. I make more than enough. But the advantages of compounding at 20% for sixty years as opposed to at 75% for ten clearly explain our differences in net worth. I also do not have sixty years ahead of me. I'll be long gone by then. Otherwise, I'd be thrilled with 20% average annualized returns.

touch it, even just a thousand becomes $128,000 at the end of the seventh year. Compounding is the one true magic the Universe has. Note that a $100 in Berkshire Hathaway in 1965 has grown to over a million dollars today. But it will be slim pickings until those years have gone by. So, either start with a lot more money than one thousand dollars, be very patient, or do something else. There are no other options. I can't help you around that, nor will I lie to you just to get your business.

Rule #6

Control Risk, the Rest Will Control Itself
(Trade and Single Account Risk)

Warren Buffett once said:

"The first rule of an investment is don't lose (money). And the second rule of an investment is don't forget the first rule. And that's all the rules there are."

Obviously, that's very Warren, very folksy, and very tongue in cheek. Also, trading isn't investing, but even if it were, Warren **has** lost money in his investments. However, he always manages to win more than he loses. So, what does he really mean?

Always control risk. Never put yourself in a position where one bad result can wipe you out. Never put yourself in a position where any one trade loses more than you decided it could lose if it doesn't work out. This is quite easily handled, by thinking of your account in terms of percentage points. For example, if you have a $5,000 account, that total is 100% of your funds. 1% of your account is thus $50. If you decide to risk 1% of your account on any one trade, then your **Maximum Allowable Loss** (memorize that term) per trade is $50. As your account grows, so does the dollar amount that represents 1% of it. Grow your account to $7,500, and continue to risk 1% per trade, only that is now $75. If your account instead drops to, say, $4,000, then you continue to risk the same 1%, but that is now $40.

Based on your Maximum Allowable Loss per trade, you would place your initial stop loss at a price point where you lose no more than 1% of your account if the trade is a loser. Control the risk, but do not limit the gain. Any one trade can produce, assuming it's a winner, 1%, 2%, 5%, 100%, or more gains. The sky's the limit! That part doesn't matter. In fact, that's the outcome you want. But you will be making those gains, always, by risking no more than 1% each time. That's how you grow an account, but more importantly, how you avoid destroying an account, when you're wrong. And believe me, you will be wrong, many times. Barring a Black Swan event, and more on those later, you can win big, but you can never lose big. Not in one single trade nor collectively, even if all open trades go bad. That last bit is the final part of this rule.

You should also have a Maximum Allowable Loss for the account itself at any one time. That will be the maximum percentage at risk on all simultaneously open trades. Going back to our 1% per trade, if I set my Maximum Allowable Loss at the account level at 5%, then I can only have 5 trades open at any one time, unless one or more of them have accrued profit and the stop loss has been moved accordingly to a price point where it is protecting gains and not preventing loss.

In other words, never, ever go all in, or you will eventually be all out. As a final note on this topic, that 1% was a suggestion, not a rule. Your Maximum Allowable Loss might be 2.5%. That's on you. Just keep in mind that the bigger you make it, the more risk you are allowing into your trading. Also, you may encounter a trade that, based on the system you are using, requires a stop loss at a price point that would exceed your Maximum Allowable loss. There are only two solutions in this case. Either trade at a smaller position size so you're within your risk control constraints, or don't take that trade!

This rule applies to the lowest level, individual trade, as well as single account risk. We will return to risk control with other rules. Risk control at all levels is your primary task if you want to succeed.

What to Do

Before you even start trading, you must take an inventory of your trading funds, in total and by trading account. For each account, the key variable is its current balance. Different traders will have different risk profiles, and these may also vary by account. Only you can decide what these are. My recommendation, though, is to never risk more than

2.5% on any single trade and no more than 20% at any one time collectively on any individual account. Beginning traders should start with lower risk profiles, for example, no more than 1% risked on any one trade and no more than 10% collectively on the account at any one time. Your maximum risk per trade determines how far away your stop loss can be. Note that it needn't be that far, it just can't be farther away than that. Adding up the individual percentages at risk at any one time also limits how many trades you can have open.[10] Of course, as your account balance grows or deceases, the percentages don't change, but the dollar amounts do. This prevents the destruction of the account during drawdowns, and compounds profits during other times.

The goal is survival. You survive by not running out of money, which allows you to still be in the game when winning trades and winning periods come along. The problem is that people are really bad at assessing risk. Doing it the way I am recommending takes subjectivity out. If you want to dig a little deeper on the subject of risk and the difficulties we humans have quantifying it, please read Luca Dellanna's excellent book on the subject, **Ergodicity: Definition, Examples, and Implications**[11].

---

[10] For example, on a $10,000 account with a maximum risk per trade of 2% and a 20% maximum collective risk, each trade can risk no more than $200, and no more than 10 $200-risking trades can be open at any one time.

[11] https://amzn.to/3UYDmeI

BOOK TWO – COMMON SENSE RULES

Rule #7

Nobody is Handing Out Free Money

I shouldn't have to write this one, but I must. I've just been asked way too many times and heard way too many horror stories to ignore it. No one is giving free money away apart from the US government in their misguided wisdom. But certainly, no legitimate broker has a viable business plan that involves giving you free money if you open an account with them, and letting you keep it. While I have seen a few reputable brokers give bonus money for deposits, usually 20%, it's usually only to a maximum of so many dollars, which come with conditions. For example, you can't just deposit $5,000, get a $1,000 bonus, and withdraw $6,000 the next day. The one reputable broker I saw doing this had the requirement of opening a minimum of 2,000 microlot trades within a 60-day period of the qualifying deposit on a minimum $1,000 account. That is the equivalent of $2,000,000 in trades. With leverage, of course, and not at the same time, but still. I don't recall ever opening even as many as a thousand trades in a single year, forget about 60 days.

And I can guarantee that if you try to open that many trades within the 60-day period, you will most likely blow up your account or, at the very least, have paid back the bonus to them in the form of spread and swap costs. And that's with a reputable broker!

The non-reputable ones, which aren't really brokers, just scam operations, will offer you even more bonus money, sometimes equal to your deposit, and they won't have any (or as many) sneaky conditions. That's because what they really want is your money. They are like the Hotel California, *you can check out any time you like, but you can never leave.*

A few years ago, a prospect who never actually got around to enrolling in my course but did spend an inordinate amount of time messaging and emailing me, told me the following. He's in Canada and had opened a trading account out of Cyprus (1st red flag) that gave him a signup bonus equal to his deposits (2nd red flag). He started trading and quickly grew his account, doubling it and tripling it, he was so good at trading (3rd red flag). He was so thrilled with his results that he sent in even more money, money he couldn't afford to lose. This is a guy who a month earlier wanted to learn trading from me, and now he thinks that his performance is blowing mine out of the water.

Now, I didn't know the entire story immediately. It came out over several conversations during a month or more. He would contact me regularly to tell me he'd made another thousand overnight trading XAUUSD (Gold vs Dollar). That alone struck me as odd, since trading gold doesn't come with leverage, it's 1:1. And I knew precisely how much gold had moved during the time he was allegedly trading it. If gold had moved $2 overnight, and he made a $1,000, he would have to have been trading 500 ounces. That was over $500,000 in margin requirement at the time (account size, with no leverage). Now, I have that size account, well, in multiple accounts, but added up, I could swing it. I never would, but I could. I'm not even a big trader, all things considered. But it still seemed odd for a beginner to have that much in play.

Long story short, he didn't have that much. He had deposited about C$30,000[12] from his life savings, received another C$30,000 as a bonus, and had grown the account, allegedly, to about C$120,000 by the time I asked him who his broker was. When he told me the name, which I forget, it was one I'd never heard of. I told him I didn't want to rain on his parade, but was he sure that it was a real broker? He said that of course it was! So, I asked him if he had ever made a withdrawal, and he said no. I asked him to do himself a favor. Withdraw C$10,000, just as a test. I told him he could always send them right back. I just wanted him to confirm that there was no problem withdrawing funds.

---

[12] Canadian dollars.

As soon as he tried to withdraw, the "company" went silent on him. No more replies to his emails, or phone calls, nothing. In a week or two, even the "broker's" website was gone. He lost every penny he had deposited, plus the bonus, plus his alleged profit. That's not all he lost, unfortunately. He lost his wife, who promptly divorced him when she found out where their life savings had gone; he lost his house to foreclosure, when he couldn't make the payments; and with the divorce, he also lost full access to his son, who he know sees on a visitation schedule.

These days, he trades solely on demo accounts, since he has no money, and he **still** contacts me sporadically! Usually, to share that he's made a killing on a demo account. Why he gets excited over making fake money is beyond me, and beyond the scope of this rule. I always tell him that I'm not doing as well as he is with my trading, but that the money I do make is real. I don't have the heart to add that I can also withdraw it whenever I want, too. Yes, I still reply, but I don't need to buy into his delusions or pretend that I do. I'm polite, but curt, and a bit sarcastic. We don't talk for long, or too often.

And I wish I could say his is the only horror story I have heard. It's not. So, please, please, do not fall for these scams. Use only reputable and well-known brokers that are licensed to operate in your country. If you have any doubts as to which these are, contact me. As the story above demonstrates, I do reply to everyone, regardless of whether they've ever paid me a dime or not. Had he thought of asking me before he did it, I would have warned him, too, for free.

Also, in general, stop looking for freebies and handouts. It's alright to grab them if you see any flying by but stop looking for them. Your business plan **cannot** have a component that relies on getting free money. You're either going to make it by trading or you're not going to make it at all.

What to Do Instead

Use your own money to trade and don't expect handouts. If you have no money, get a job, save up, and only then trade. Use the time it's going to take to amass some trading capital to learn. And only use reputable brokers regulated by US or EU authorities. There are many scams out there, but every single one relies on the victim being both greedy and naive. Don't be either one.

Rule #8

The Market isn't Going Anywhere

Really. It will be here tomorrow. Unless today is Friday, in which case, it'll be back in a couple of days. Most beginners, and even some seasoned traders, suffer from must-tradeitis. They think they must always be in a trade or they're not really traders. This is a huge misconception. It's perfectly fine to be all cash at times. In fact, during certain market conditions, it's best to be all cash. It's certainly better to be out of the market than to be in trades you shouldn't be in, and that's the key. I have mentioned several times already that you must have a system. A system will tell you what to trade, when to trade it, how much to trade, how much to risk, and when to get out. More importantly, if your system is not signaling a trade, then it's implicitly telling you NOT to trade.

Some of the systems I use only give an entry signal a few times a year, if that, but when they do! When they do, they usually hit it out of the ballpark. Some of those rare entry signals are responsible for a good chunk of my yearly profits. But they can't be forced. For months on end, it might be signaling no trade. Of course, that's one system out of several that I use, a very long term, trend following system. I have other systems that are medium term, giving slightly more frequent signals, and I very rarely trade short term, but those might signal daily or even more often.

I sometimes go entire weeks without getting an entry signal. Sometimes I'll have open trades I'm managing, other times I'll be all cash. When it's the latter, I will check the charts once every day or two, and I will focus on my activities outside the markets. To be honest, even when there are entry signals and/or open trades, I don't spend more than 10 to 15 minutes a day trading. But what I most definitely will not do is force a trade just to be in a trade.

If you have the pressing psychological need to be in a trade, I suggest you work on that. There is no urgency, the market isn't going anywhere, and FOMO[13] should not be part of your toolbox. Be patient, trust your systems, and follow them, to the letter. You are not going to catch every market move, no one does, no one can. And you don't need to. Catch enough of them, though, and you're set, financially speaking. Get into too many suboptimal trades because you're impatient, and that will have a devastating effect on your results. Remember, it's always better to regret not being in a trade, than to regret being in one.

---

[13] Fear Of Missing Out.

What to Do

This one's simple. Have a *trading system*. Only take trades signaled by your system and follow your risk parameters strictly. That last piece is important. Even a valid signal should and has to be ignored if you already have too many open trades and adding one violates your Maximum Allowable Risk at the account level, or individually, if the necessary stop loss is beyond your maximum allowed risk per individual trade.

Rule #9

You Don't Need to Win 51% of the Time or More in Order to be Successful

Rule #2 already made it clear that we can't win on every trade, this rule will show you that you don't even need to win most of the time in order to have a successful trading career. I once admitted on an online forum that I am right (meaning that I end up with a winning trade) only 30% of the time, and that still allows me to double or come close to doubling my money every year.

Some forum know-it-all, and don't you love those, snidely pointed out that he could do better tossing a coin and being right half the time. In Spanish there's a saying, *"la ignorancia es atrevida"*, which translates roughly to, *"ignorance is brazenly outspoken"*. I explained to this "expert" that trading isn't a coin toss. It doesn't have a binary outcome in which you can only win or lose a fixed sum. If we were playing a game of chance with a binary outcome, for $1 each throw, then winning half the time would be a break even situation. In such a scenario, I would need to win at least half of the games plus 1 to start showing a profit. If I win 60% of the time, now we're cooking with gas!

But trading isn't like that. Trading doesn't have a binary outcome. I can lose $5 in one trade and win $25 in the next trade. I could stop there, having won half of the time, and show a net $20 profit. Or I could make ten trades, lose $5 each on seven trades, win $25 each on the remaining three, giving me a 30% win rate, and still show a net $40 profit. Which was precisely the point I was making in my story above, and which whooshed right over the know-it-all's head.

It's also the point behind this rule. Certainly, your win rate is important, but far more important is how much your winners win versus how much your losers lose. This is what will really make or break you. You can lose 9 times out of 10, if the individual losses are small, and still retire rich if that 10th trade is a huge winner that makes up for the losses and then some. And, assuming you are consistent in both your win rate, average loss, and average win, just keep repeating what you're doing. Or, to steal a line from the shampoo industry, **lather, rinse, repeat**.

So, combining this rule and Rule #2, I guess we could say, you can't win all the time, and you don't even need to win most of the time. Make sure you understand this. A lot of the people who fail at trading are looking for the wrong kind of edge. Trading is one of the few endeavors where you can be mostly wrong all the way to the top, statistically speaking, of course.

I've also seen people with high win rates, say 75%, who still consistently lost money. Why? Because their losers were bigger than their winners, by a lot (See Rules #3 and #4).

What to Do Instead

I know, I'm getting repetitive, but it's the truth. Have a *trading system* that minimizes amounts lost and maximizes amounts won (amounts, not individual trades). That, combined with proper *risk control*, will put you over the top **over time**. Remember, it's alright to have losing periods. In fact, you **will** have losing periods. But, over longer periods of time, your account should grow. If it's not growing, then it's time to reassess your approach, your systems, or your risk control. Perhaps all of them.

BOOK THREE – SOME MATH RULES

Rule #10

Long Term Outperforms Short Term

This will be true almost always. Markets don't move steadily in a single direction. Instead, they zig and they zag. How long you keep a trade open will usually determine what you expect of it. In the forex market, potential gains per trade will be, as a rule of thumb:

- Scalping (trades open anywhere from seconds to minutes) - 5 to 30 pips
- Intraday Trading (trades opened and closed the same day) - 30 to 100 pips
- Swing Trading (trades open anywhere from days to weeks) - 100 to 300 pips
- Position (Trend) Trading (trades open weeks, months, or years) 300 to 1000s of pips

Since the market is zigging and zagging, it stands to reason that the shorter the timeframe, the smaller these zigs and zags will be, which explains the differences in potential gains. Additionally, the closer you are to the scalping end of the spectrum, the more time you will need to spend staring at your screen and scanning for opportunities. Scalpers might be in and out of the market dozens or more times a day. That means that they will usually spend hours every day in front of their consoles. Those trading the other end of the spectrum might only need to be scanning the market daily, or even weekly. When they do so, it rarely takes them more than a half hour or so to determine whether there are any opportunities.

There is nothing wrong with any of these approaches. Some people will simply be better suited for one or more of them, temperamentally or for other reasons. Personally, I can't scalp. Oh, I know how to do it and I'm quite good at it. I just can't sit in front of my trading console for 6-8 hours a day, no matter how much extra money I'd make. I would be miserable. My sweet spots are swing and positional trading, and I only look at the charts once every day or two, and never for more than an hour. I do keep tabs on open trades daily, but even then, I'll be relying more on my adjusted or trailing stops to keep me safe than on my monitoring. I monitor because I enjoy doing so, more than for any other reason. I'm human, too, and it does little harm.

But long story short, a scalper will work much harder for 300 pips than will a position trader, but the scalper can probably make more pips over the same period of time it takes the position trader to make his 300. A scalper might make 300 pips every day or two, whereas it might take a week or more for the position trader to make the same 300 pips. Position traders, however, are usually working with more capital, making their pips far more valuable than the scalper's. There are always trade-offs.

What to Do

There really isn't a wrong approach here. What you do need to do is know yourself, your temperament, and your skills. When starting out, keep an open mind and try out all types of trading, always with a system and risk control backing you up. Identify which style or styles suit you best and focus your energy on those. Don't compare yourself to other traders. Learn from others and adopt or adapt what they're doing, but only to the point that it matches your strengths and preferences. A scalper might triple my yearly results. Or not. Either way, they aren't my competition nor my yardstick. The important thing is to identify the trading style that best suits you, and get the best trading results out of it that you can. Many otherwise excellent traders fail or stumble because they're trying to do things that go against their grain. Your only true competition is yourself. Get better at trading every day. That's enough.

Rule #11

You Will Not Get Rich Overnight

Trading successfully isn't a matter of being right in a big way one time and retiring. Trading is like any other business. Even the most successful traditional businesses have gradual, cumulative revenue. Walmart did not open a store, sell everything in it once, and allow Sam Walton to retire. Trading is the same. If you want to be rich overnight, consider the lottery There, at least, it's improbable to the extreme, but it's still statistically possible.

With trading, however, assuming you do things right, you're going to find your account balance growing very slowly. %1 up one week, 2% down the next. Then 1% up again, then a good run may take you 10% up in the following few weeks. Congrats. You've reached a slight but noticeably higher account balance. And then the cycle starts all over again. After a year, you might have doubled your account. Maintaining your established risk levels, you can now open somewhat larger trades, or open twice as many trades at the same position size as before.

Either one is going to improve your gains, if your system is working. And it is working, right? You doubled that account. But it still took a year. If things go well, after another year, you may have doubled your account again. This time, it's even more significant, because even though you only doubled it from the prior year, it's now 4 times bigger than when you started, thanks to doubling it twice. Do it again, and now it's 8 times bigger. But 3 years have gone by. But you see how growth accelerates?

People who understand this will gain momentum over long periods of time, even if they have a negative year occasionally. Those who come in with the intention of making a killing quickly will not achieve it, nor will they have the slow but steady gains described above. You can't pursue both, and by pursuing the one that's unattainable, you will also forgo the one that could have been attained.

You will read stories of amazing wins, and some of them are even legitimate. Don't let them fool or distract you.

For example, George Soros is known as **The Man Who Broke the Bank of England**. He didn't, but it sounds cool. What he did do was make a massive bet against the British Pound at a time when England was keeping their currency artificially pegged to the Deutsche Mark. Soros intelligently and correctly determined that the Bank of England couldn't sustain the artificial price, and that when they gave in, it would move violently. He believed in the idea so strongly that he risked a few hundred million dollars placing a trade in the direction he expected. And then he waited. It still wasn't overnight. It was months. But, finally, the Bank of England was forced to capitulate, Soros made just about a billion dollars, and he acquired a cool nickname. But let's not forget that a) he had a few hundred million dollars and b) he was willing to put them on the line. Had he been wrong, he would have lost those few hundred million dollars. That was the combination of having a keen ability to identify an unsustainable situation, access to capital, and a high risk tolerance. Let's also not forget that by placing a few hundred million down, his gain was about 3 times his account size. In other words, he tripled his account. He didn't make a billion from a few thousand dollars.

You may also hear about the bookish nerd (or many of them) who sagely believed in Bitcoin and bought or mined a few hundred of them back when they were worth a dollar. This, too, is true. It happened. But a) it took a years and b) it was more luck than insight. I'm sorry to disappoint any crypto enthusiasts reading me, but cryptocurrencies are not backed by anyone and have no actual value. They are worth whatever the last guy paid for them, and the next guy might decide to pay 100 times less, or maybe 100 times more. But there's no rhyme nor reason. You might say that a dollar has no real value, either, and I won't argue, but at least it is backed by the government of the United States of America, who accepts them in payment of debts, public and private, etc. So, the Bitcoin people have enjoyed amazing luck and substantial profit, assuming they entered at a good price, and held on throughout all the turmoil, or got out at one of its highs. Its volatility is a testament to what I said above, it being worth whatever the next guy wants to pay, and sometimes one guy and the next produce swings of thousands of dollars, with crashes between 50 and 95% happening within days.

For every Soros who took big risks and was amply paid or every enthusiast with a strong belief in something new who is proved right, there's a million others who lost the capital they put at risk and/or had their belief come to naught. The problem is that you only hear about the handful who struck pay-dirt. The rest are never mentioned, unsung victims of harsh reality. You also never hear about the guy who grew his money 25% every year and retires richer than Rockefeller, because that's a boring story.

Extra! Extra! Read all about it! Man becomes rich over 20 years!

No, I don't think that would sell newspapers.

So, can you get rich quickly? Not the way Soros did it, that wasn't quick, and besides, he was already rich, using his wealth to make more money. If he'd only had a $100 to his name, he'd have still won the trade, but only tripled his stake to $300. You can strike it rich, though, and perhaps even overnight, by buying the right crypto at a very, very low price just before the next boom. But that and buying a lottery ticket sound about the same. You're hoping for luck to strike.

So, back to trading, no, it's not going to happen. If you want to become rich without being rich to begin with, it's going to take time. That's why the best time to start was yesterday, and the next best time is today.

What to Do Instead

Look for consistent gains over long periods of time, peppered by the odd large gain every now and then. It all goes back to what we said about expectations. The market is no place for the impatient, but if you have the skills, the consistency, and the time, a large account may become massive, and even a small account becomes a large account. To do this, risk control must be your primary concern. Risk too much, and you will lose too much. You can undo years of profit with one bad trade. Many have, and their stories are worth reading[14], as cautionary tales. Don't focus only on the success stories or you'll miss half the picture.

---

[14] https://amzn.to/4a85b8K

Rule #12

Compounding is Your Best Friend

This was hinted at in the prior rule. Remember that doubling, and redoubling? That's compounding. It is truly magical. Double your money twice, and you don't have twice the money, you have quadruple the money. Do it again, and you have 8 times the original amount. One more time, and it's 16 times. Again, 32 times. Let's see what happens to a small amount not even doubled, just grown 50% a year over 20 years.

Example of Compounding Over 20 Years

Year	Starting Balance	Deposit	Gain	Ending Balance
1	$ 1,000.00		$ 500.00	$ 1,500.00
2	$ 1,500.00		$ 750.00	$ 2,250.00
3	$ 2,250.00		$ 1,125.00	$ 3,375.00
4	$ 3,375.00		$ 1,687.50	$ 5,062.50
5	$ 5,062.50		$ 2,531.25	$ 7,593.75
6	$ 7,593.75		$ 3,796.88	$ 11,390.63
7	$ 11,390.63		$ 5,695.31	$ 17,085.94
8	$ 17,085.94		$ 8,542.97	$ 25,628.91
9	$ 25,628.91		$ 12,814.45	$ 38,443.36

10	$	38,443.36	$	19,221.68	$	57,665.04
11	$	57,665.04	$	28,832.52	$	86,497.56
12	$	86,497.56	$	43,248.78	$	129,746.34
13	$	129,746.34	$	64,873.17	$	194,619.51
14	$	194,619.51	$	97,309.75	$	291,929.26
15	$	291,929.26	$	145,964.63	$	437,893.89
16	$	437,893.89	$	218,946.95	$	656,840.84
17	$	656,840.84	$	328,420.42	$	985,261.25
18	$	985,261.25	$	492,630.63	$	1,477,891.88
19	$	1,477,891.88	$	738,945.94	$	2,216,837.82
20	$	2,216,837.82	$	1,108,418.91	$	3,325,256.73

US$3.3 million, starting with an even US$1,000, and not adding even a penny along the way. Just trading relatively safely (there is always risk when trading), looking for only 50% a year. Very doable. You also don't need to stop after 20 years, though I would strongly suggest you seek lower returns via less risky instruments by then, but that's up to you. Notice, however, that more than US$3 million of those gains happened in the final 6 years. Compounding really shines towards the end, if not as much for most of its initial run. This can be frustrating for some people.

Of course, if you start with US$50,000, the numbers near the bottom would have a hard time fitting on the page.

Example of Compounding Over 20 Years

Year	Starting Balance	Deposit	Gain	Ending Balance
1	$ 50,000.00		$ 25,000.00	$ 75,000.00
2	$ 75,000.00		$ 37,500.00	$ 112,500.00
3	$ 112,500.00		$ 56,250.00	$ 168,750.00
4	$ 168,750.00		$ 84,375.00	$ 253,125.00
5	$ 253,125.00		$ 126,562.50	$ 379,687.50
6	$ 379,687.50		$ 189,843.75	$ 569,531.25
7	$ 569,531.25		$ 284,765.63	$ 854,296.88
8	$ 854,296.88		$ 427,148.44	$ 1,281,445.31
9	$ 1,281,445.31		$ 640,722.66	$ 1,922,167.97
10	$ 1,922,167.97		$ 961,083.98	$ 2,883,251.95
11	$ 2,883,251.95		$ 1,441,625.98	$ 4,324,877.93
12	$ 4,324,877.93		$ 2,162,438.96	$ 6,487,316.89
13	$ 6,487,316.89		$ 3,243,658.45	$ 9,730,975.34
14	$ 9,730,975.34		$ 4,865,487.67	$ 14,596,463.01
15	$ 14,596,463.01		$ 7,298,231.51	$ 21,894,694.52
16	$ 21,894,694.52		$ 10,947,347.26	$ 32,842,041.78
17	$ 32,842,041.78		$ 16,421,020.89	$ 49,263,062.67
18	$ 49,263,062.67		$ 24,631,531.33	$ 73,894,594.00
19	$ 73,894,594.00		$ 36,947,297.00	$ 110,841,891.00
20	$ 110,841,891.00		$ 55,420,945.50	$ 166,262,836.50

A similar value explosion would happen if you started with the original US$1,000 but added money every year. We end up with US$10 million. $6 million and change more than if we hadn't added any money, and we only added US$19,000 along the way, in US$1,000 annual boosts. That's the premise behind 401(k)s, IRAs, and similar retirement plans. Start small, add every period, and compound.

Example of Compounding Over 20 Years

Year	Starting Balance	Deposit	Gain	Ending Balance
1	$ 1,000.00		$ 500.00	$ 1,500.00
2	$ 1,500.00	$ 1,000.00	$ 1,250.00	$ 3,750.00
3	$ 3,750.00	$ 1,000.00	$ 2,375.00	$ 7,125.00
4	$ 7,125.00	$ 1,000.00	$ 4,062.50	$ 12,187.50
5	$ 12,187.50	$ 1,000.00	$ 6,593.75	$ 19,781.25
6	$ 19,781.25	$ 1,000.00	$ 10,390.63	$ 31,171.88
7	$ 31,171.88	$ 1,000.00	$ 16,085.94	$ 48,257.81
8	$ 48,257.81	$ 1,000.00	$ 24,628.91	$ 73,886.72
9	$ 73,886.72	$ 1,000.00	$ 37,443.36	$ 112,330.08
10	$ 112,330.08	$ 1,000.00	$ 56,665.04	$ 169,995.12
11	$ 169,995.12	$ 1,000.00	$ 85,497.56	$ 256,492.68
12	$ 256,492.68	$ 1,000.00	$ 128,746.34	$ 386,239.01
13	$ 386,239.01	$ 1,000.00	$ 193,619.51	$ 580,858.52
14	$ 580,858.52	$ 1,000.00	$ 290,929.26	$ 872,787.78
15	$ 872,787.78	$ 1,000.00	$ 436,893.89	$ 1,310,681.67
16	$ 1,310,681.67	$ 1,000.00	$ 655,840.84	$ 1,967,522.51
17	$ 1,967,522.51	$ 1,000.00	$ 984,261.25	$ 2,952,783.76
18	$ 2,952,783.76	$ 1,000.00	$ 1,476,891.88	$ 4,430,675.64
19	$ 4,430,675.64	$ 1,000.00	$ 2,215,837.82	$ 6,647,513.46

| 20 | $ 6,647,513.46 | $ 1,000.00 | $ 3,324,256.73 | $ 9,972,770.19 |

Always keep the end result in mind. Patience and staying the course are rewarded. The reason compounding works, of course, is that money isn't taken out. The same percentage, 50% in the examples above, is working every consecutive year with increasingly larger amounts of money.

What to Do

First, learn. Once you're operating consistently, start trading with as much capital as you care to risk. Add to it as often as you can. Let it grow. Avoid taking any out for as long as you can, and let it compound. If you're doing it right, there will come a point where it stops making sense to risk so much on what is, no matter how good you are, a high risk venture. Judiciously start moving some of the profits into lower return investments with lower risk. A guaranteed 15% a year on a million dollars can be better than a possible 100% on the same money but where you might lose half of it. Whereas 15% on $10,000 isn't as attractive, and doubling that money, even at higher risk, is just good business sense.

BOOK FOUR – GENERAL TRADING RULES

Rule #13

Trends Are Your Other Best Friend

In a prior rule, we mentioned how the market, regardless of the time frame, moves in zigs and zags. You can see this on a 5-minute chart of the EURUSD:

And you can see it on a daily chart of the same EURUSD:

Both charts terminate at the current date and time as I write this and show the same price within less than a pip, what the market moved between my taking the two snapshots. Notice how they both zig and zag over time, with price weaving up and down, but also often sustaining a single direction for many candles. These sustained movements are trends. Periods when the market is consistently moving in a single direction. Also notice that in the 5-minute chart, the longest trends, and only a few of those, are perhaps 50 pips long. Whereas in the daily chart, you can see a trend running for hundreds of pips.

These trends are what you need to look for when trading. Not every entry will result in a winning trade, but trends will give you your biggest winners, if you don't jump the gun and exit too quickly. Risk a *little* even if it doesn't work out and be ready to lose that *little* multiple times. Then catch a trend, win big, make up for the small losses, and then some. Repeat.

You need to identify a potential trend when it starts, and this is where your trading systems come in, and identify when the trend has run its course, and is turning around, essentially, starting a trend in the opposite direction. Which you can also trade! You're trying to ride every zig and every zag, knowing only a few will be big winners. And *a big winner* means a different number of pips in different time frames.

Trends are your second best friend until they end!

What to Do

Learn technical analysis. This will allow you to identify trends, turnarounds, and other opportunities in the charts. Use a trading system with clear rules on what to do based on what's in the charts. Not all trading systems are trend following[15] ones, but you will find that most of them are. A good trend lasts for many candles (periods) in whatever timeframe you're analyzing. Stay in a successful trend trade for as long as possible. These will always be your big winners.

---

[15] https://amzn.to/3ViucJQ

Rule #14

Trading is Boring, Except When it Isn't

If you're doing trading right, you will be bored 99% of the time. It's going to be endless looking at charts, waiting for entries, not seeing any, repeating, repeating, repeating. Depending on your trading style, scalping through position trading, you might spend hours to weeks waiting for an entry. And then, suddenly, all hell breaks loose and you're busy, and then it all goes back to boring not too long after.

That's what you want. If you're looking for thrills, if you're an adrenaline junkie, you should not trade. It's not going to end well for you. And, even when all hell does break loose, you want to be calm and collected. While others panic, you want to be operating like a well-oiled machine, and just as mechanically.

Your emotions shouldn't be telling you what to do, it's your systems that should be in control. I cannot stress this enough, treat trading like a business. Businesses should be boring, they should be somewhat predictable, and even the uncertainties should be somewhat planned for. You may not know that something will happen, but you should already know what to do if something like it does happen. Surprises are bad things. In a traditional business, things usually get very exciting when very bad things are happening to or inside the business. Only rarely do surprises end up being good for the business.

Same thing with trading. We cannot know what's going to happen, but we know that eventually something will happen. Our systems, risk control, capital assignments, and everything else need to be ready to go.

- The EURUSD broke out of its range - Your trading system should trigger an entry, an exit, or a do nothing.
- Your capital dropped by 10% due to a string of bad trades - Your risk control and capital allocation procedures should tell you what to do.
- War broke out in the Middle East - Your trading plan should have procedures in place for the resultant volatility.
- Your broker went Chapter 11 - You have more than one broker, right? Right?
- You lost your Internet connection - You should have backups for all your critical devices and communications.
- You're laid up in the hospital with the screaming heebie-jeebies - You have a plan for that.
- Civil unrest, looting, and arson broke out in your neighborhood - You need to have a plan for that.

- Aliens landed - You have a plan for that.

Yes, I'm starting to get ridiculous, and facetious, and I might just be grasping at straws. But many of the things that might happen will eventually happen, and you should have a plan for them. I can guarantee that everything on that list has a greater than zero chance of happening anytime between the next few minutes to sometime within your active trading career, except for that last one. And, even then, I wouldn't say there's no chance. I only scratched the surface of the list of possible events. You'll want to be a lot more thorough.

What to Do

The takeaway is that you need to consider everything that might happen and have a plan to deal with it. From the very small everyday things, to the once in a lifetime (you hope) event. If something never actually happens, you didn't lose anything, but if it does, boy, will you be glad you had a plan, a backup, or an alternate way out of the building.

Take some time to think about this and write it all down. If your plans aren't on paper, or easily accessible on a computer, they're not plans, they're fuzzy imaginings.

Rule #15

You Can't Have Quotas

This is one I get a lot. People ask me how much they're going to make each week if they learn from me. Trading doesn't come with a salary. You're not going to get a weekly paycheck. It's not a job, unless you're working for a hedge fund, of course, Then it is a job, with a salary and bonuses, but you don't get to keep the profits you generate; you're an employee.

The reality of trading is that I have no idea how much I am going to make this week, this month, this quarter, this semester, or even this year. All I can do is look at my past performance, which hopefully has some consistency, and hope that this year looks like the last or better. But guess what? This year could very well be a loser. We're back to Rule #1, you cannot predict the market, hence you cannot predict how much you'll make.

If you're doing things right, you should be making money yearly, and it should be compounding. But thinking that every week is going to be a 1% gain just because last year you came in at 68% gains for the year is unrealistic and dangerous. People who have quotas start getting very nervous towards the end of the period if they're not meeting them. That's when they start doing stupid things.

I once worked for a very powerful telecommunications equipment manufacturer, Nortel Networks. Nortel was exceeding market expectations, thanks to a stellar research and development division, great products far ahead of the competition, and a wonderful relationship with their sales channels. Nortel dominated the PBX, Telephony, Switch, and Cellular Network market in the mid to late nineties.

Then they flew too close to the Sun, exactly like Icarus. At the end of the nineties, the tech bubble burst. Technology had overreached, too many networks had been deployed, too much fiber had been laid down in expectation of ever rising bandwidth demands which suddenly dried up. Tech stocks crashed and companies disappeared. Nortel, instead of taking its lumps, started cooking the books. They sent equipment to sales channels that they knew was not going to be sold. Don't worry, they told their vendors, we just need to shore up our sales numbers this quarter. You can return the equipment without paying anything next month. Nortel's sales numbers boomed as everyone else's were crashing.

Obviously, that wasn't sustainable. The revenue never came in, and all those reported sales were, eventually, returned and canceled. Even more cooking of the books happened behind closed doors, but it was too late. Nortel went into bankruptcy, taking most of Canada's pension system with it, and no longer exists[16].

All because someone felt quotas had to be met. Don't ever do that. In trading, those who need to meet quotas will start taking bigger and bigger risks, hoping to make the week or, with even greater desperation, to not end up in the red for the week, the month, or even the year.

You. Will. Have. Losing. Periods.

Eventually, you will even have a losing year if you don't have a few of those right out of the gate. Trading is not for the faint of heart. We take bigger risks than the general public, who only need to get up in the morning and clock in at work to guarantee a paycheck, but we have the ability to make multiples of their average salary. With risk comes the possibility of loss, and where there is a possibility greater than zero, it will eventually happen.

It will happen even quicker and more often if you think you must meet a quota. Having expectations is one thing, thinking the market owes you a salary is something else entirely.

---

[16] https://www.cbc.ca/news/business/canada-s-technology-star-becomes-financial-black-hole-1.782655

Instead, what will happen is that with consistency, you will attain annualized average returns of x%. The emphasis there is on annualized and average. If my annualized returns are at 80%, that can mean I make exactly 80% each year (unlikely, but it could happen), or that I lost 50% last year and was up 224% this year, or a million other combinations. I kept it simple by only doing 2 years but, of course, annualized averages for anything less than a decade are meaningless. Not enough data.

Just remember, if you do lose 50% of your account, you then need to have 100% gains just to get back to where you were before the loss. That's why the example above with the 50% loss required 224% the second year to achieve 80% gains averaged yearly. The more you lose, the harder it is to recover. At some point, you can't. Leaving you with 2 options. Quit or add more money to your dead account.

What to Do Instead

Having quotas is thus both unrealistic and dangerous because they lead to bad habits and bad trading. Trade every day the same as any other, following your systems, and keeping track of your gains or losses by the penny and by percentages. If profits are coming in, carefully see if they can be improved. If they can, do so, over time. If losses are piling up, figure out why and fix it. Maybe you're using the wrong system for current market conditions. Maybe it's a bad system that just happened to perform well for a time. Maybe you're at fault. Whatever it is, STOP. Reassess, correct, and start again.

Rule #16

Trade Broadly, Trade Often

Don't get me wrong, overtrading is bad. Like really bad. In fact, that will be its own rule. But you also cannot win at trading if you're not opening enough trades. Or trading as broadly in the market as is safely possible. Sure, you can specialize and only trade the Euro against the Dollar, but what happens if that pair just isn't giving you enough opportunities/entries? Or what happens if there's a sustained period of wrong signals on that pair from your system? This is the **broad**. Trade as many pairs as you can, and you'll be far more likely to find a trading opportunity at any given time. If one pair isn't performing, there will be ten others that are.

For the odds to be in your favor, you must have enough properly triggered trades for those odds to work with. Throw a coin and tabulate the heads vs tails that come up. If you throw the coin ten times, you will only rarely and by pure chance get five heads and five tails. Not enough throws for the odds to work. You may even get a run of ten heads. But flip that coin ten thousand times, and you're far more likely to come very close to five thousand heads and five thousand tails. Better yet, find ten thousand coins and flip them all at once. It'll be quicker, and you'll still come very close to a fifty-fifty split. This is the **often**.

Trade enough things, enough times, following the rules, mind you, and you'll find opportunities galore that will allow the odds to work in your favor.

Now, if you are scanning the charts for opportunities, and finding them, but not taking them all, that's a problem. One that needs to be fixed. If it's something psychological, work on it. If I see 25 entries at one time, I'll take all 25, assuming they don't violate any of my risk parameters. If you can't take them because there's not enough margin in your account, then you are undercapitalized. That is dangerous, in and of itself, but in this case, it will also prevent you from stacking those odds in your favor. And you always want the odds stacked in your favor. Always. You can either lower your trading lot size, if that's possible, or add more money to the account.

If you can't add more money to the account, in that last scenario, you will be at a severe disadvantage. Trading is not the place where you want to be under disadvantages, trust me on that. But if that is the case, your primary objective will, or should be, really, to get more capital.

What to Do

You need to be positioned, psychologically and financially, to trade as many opportunities as your trading system presents in as many currency pairs as possible, provided it doesn't violate your risk parameters. For the odds to favor you, you need to give them a field to operate in. It's the law of large numbers. Trading is ergodic[17] if you don't suffer a catastrophic failure along the way. For optimal results to come in, however, you must trade enough times for the odds to play out.

---

[17] A system has ergodicity if it performs equally in series as well as in parallel. For example, flipping a coin ten thousand times should yield a similar result to flipping ten thousand coins all at once, if coin flipping is ergodic. Which it is.

Rule #17

Don't Overtrade

Overtrading takes many forms. All are bad. Essentially, it means taking trades that you shouldn't have taken. If you are following a system, then the worst forms of overtrading are covered. Overleveraging, however, might still be a problem. Let's cover the most common, while keeping the essential definition in mind as a general caution.

1. Overleveraging through too many open positions - This is one that you can only avoid if you have sufficient trading capital. Let's start with the assumption that you are following a trading system, because otherwise overleveraging is the least of your problems. Your trading system, scanning just the major pairs (crosses between the USD, EUR, GBP, JPY, CHF, AUD, and NZD) will generate entries with a certain regularity, anywhere between dozens at a time and from there down. For a trading system to work properly, you MUST take every single entry presented, as covered in other rules. The problem is that every trade you open uses up some of your margin, and unless you are

sufficiently capitalized, you will eventually run out of margin, or leave yourself vulnerable to a margin call, if the market temporarily moves against you. Most traders are undercapitalized when starting out. As a rule of thumb, you should never use more than 75% of your margin at any given time and, preferably, you should not exceed 50%. This gives you ample breathing room to get through temporary downturns in your open trades.

2. Overleveraging through position size - Similar to the above, but instead of too many open trades, it is trading at too large a position size. When a trading system is enjoying a good run, that is, a period of better than usual performance, or simply because a trader gets impatient and wants to have greater potential gains, there comes the temptation to trade at higher position sizes than is safe for the account. We covered in risk control how the Maximum Allowable Risk per trade dictates the stop loss and, to a great extent, the position size. This, in turn, determines the amount to be won or lost per pip of movement. Trading at higher position sizes than warranted increases the risk. It may result in greater gains, temporarily, but you will be giving those back, and then some, as soon as the system's performance reverts to the mean, or market volatility turns against you. Any trading system

with improper risk control is a disaster waiting to happen, and you often won't have to wait long.

3. Any Form of "Discretionary Trading" - Some traders will disagree with me, thinking that the most exalted traders, past and present, have some sort of sixth sense such that they can "see" a winning trade and be almost always right. This is half Hollywood hype and half wishful thinking. While some great traders do call themselves "discretionary traders", they always have some sort of criteria that picks their trades for them. In other words, a trading system. Perhaps it's not formally written down or doesn't rely solely or at all on technical analysis "charting", but it's there, in their heads, or that trader is going to have a very short and painful career. The oversized faith some less experienced traders have in their imagined innate abilities, though, makes some of them override their systems or not use one at all. Trust me, I have interacted with many professional traders and the odd Market Wizard[18].

---

[18] https://amzn.to/3UZV1CB - Market Wizards is a highly recommended series of books written by Jack D. Schwager, where he interviews some of the most successful traders of the past half century through today. Full disclosure, a handful of them have blown up since their interviews, but not that many. And the lessons they reveal remain valid, either way. You will find, if you read them, that every trader interviewed has a specific way of doing things that

Not even one is a "discretionary trader". They all have a system or multiple systems, though some might be very secretive and deny it.
4. Boredom - Sometimes, there are no trades. The market is sideways, or for whatever reason, your trading system isn't signaling any entries. This can go on for hours, days, even weeks, depending on your system's timeframe. Some traders feel that they must be always in a trade or they're not traders. Sometimes, they try to anticipate their system. It might be presenting 5 out of the 6 necessary conditions to enter a trade. Close enough, right? No. You either follow a system or you don't. Following a system 99% of the time is the same as not following the system. If there are no valid entries, don't let boredom control you. Go do something else. It is better not to be in any trades than to be in bad trades.

What to Do Instead

Once again, you MUST have a system and you MUST follow it. You MUST have proper risk control and cannot

---

they attribute their success to. No two traders are alike, but they still share commonalities, and if you catalog them, you might find that they closely resemble the contents of this book, except mine is more to the point and compact.

change those conditions on the fly. Together, they make up your trading plan, which is the equivalent of your Operations Manual, if you were a brick and mortar business. These are the things that differentiate you from a dabbler or a hobby trader. They are the things that will keep you safe and, in the market, profitably, for years to come. Diverging even slightly from this may work out for you here and there, even for extended periods, but will also guarantee your inevitable failure and loss of your trading capital. Diverging totally from this will quickly be catastrophic.

Rule #18

Trade with a System, Always

We've mentioned trading systems in more than half the Rules, and even given snippets of them, but we haven't fully defined what constitutes a trading system. That was by design. While they are mandatory and necessary, we had to set up the ground rules first. Now we can get into some of the more complex rules. If you've made it this far into the book, you're already ahead of almost every other novice trader out there.

The problem with most novice traders, and unfortunately, many more experienced traders who should know better, is that they fly by the seat of their pants. They're forever looking for that big score, the next big thing, chasing tips they've picked up on the Internet, or perhaps, from their barber, idea after crappy idea. Maybe they even have what they think are superior abilities to "sense" good trades. If they're unlucky, then one of those actually works out, after which they're forever seeking to repeat it, confident that if they did it once, they can do it again. We all think we're better than the average which, statistically speaking, is impossible. There's even a name for it, the Dunning Kruger Effect[19]. And we all think we're the exception.

Some traders will even bet the farm, so to speak, looking for the outsized gains that can only come from going all in. They'll risk more than they should, because why not? Since there was no entry strategy, why bother with an exit strategy, either? So, they also won't be consistent in getting out. It's the dictionary definition of winging it. They saw a movie or read a book, where some guy had a brilliant idea and rode it into the sunset. They don't realize that for every guy who had such an idea that worked, there are a million others who lost it all. Of course, they don't write books or make movies about those guys. You only get to see the 1 in a million who won against all odds, like in the movie, The Big Short[20]. Again, it **can** happen. It's just **not likely** to happen.

What is likely to happen is that, provided you are following a system, you will make steady and consistent gains. It won't be spectacular. It might look boring on paper. But even making a boring 1% a week comes out to about 68% a year, thanks to compounding. That's better than 99% of mutual funds, hedge funds, trading outfits, and specialty traders. Heck, it's better than Warren Buffett. Note that Buffett isn't a trader, he's an investor, so the comparison

---

[19] The Dunning–Kruger effect is a very prevalent cognitive bias in which people with limited competence in a particular domain overestimate their abilities.

[20] https://amzn.to/49M3Wfu

isn't fair. He's not high risk, traders are. Traders must be, if they're looking for 68% a year or better, year after year.

Be boring. Have a system. Leave the excitement for the guys that go broke every year chasing after the next Big Short, or the next Bitcoin at 13 cents.

What to Do

Have a system. But what constitutes a system? A system is a set of rules and conditions that tells you what to trade, when to trade it, how to adjust open trades, and when to close them. Every possible decision that can present itself, from opening a trade to finally closing it must be covered by the trading system. This does not include position sizing or any other aspect of risk control except in the most rudimentary and mechanical fashion. Your overall risk control parameters and overall trading plan oversee that, and have greater weight than any trading system, which becomes a component of your plan.

In the general scheme of things, it will look like this:

A. Global and Inviolable Risk Control Parameters
    a. 1st Account-based and Inviolable Risk Parameters
        i. Account-based trading system 1
        ii. Account-based trading system 2

    iii. Account-based trading system 3
  b. 2nd Account-based and Inviolable Risk Parameters
    i. Account-based trading system 1
    ii. Account-based trading system 2
    iii. Account-based trading system 3
  c. 3rd Account-based and Inviolable Risk Parameters
    i. Account-based trading system 1
    ii. Account-based trading system 2
    iii. Account-based trading system 3
  d. And as many more entries as you choose to have accounts for.

  Note that the system or systems used within each account can be completely different from other accounts, as can be their risk parameters, if they don't violate the Global Risk Parameters. You also should not use more than one system simultaneously on any one account but may use a different one at different times. The hierarchy provides a framework that is consistent and repeatable. It moves trading out of the art column and into the science column. Also worth pointing out is that if you only have one account and one trading system, then your entire framework will simply consist of lines A, a, and i. That's perfectly fine.

  An example trading system, and we will give actual trading systems in the appendices, may tell you that if a forex pair makes a new 20-day high in price, go long (and if it's a 20-day low in price, go short), setting the initial stop loss at twice the 20-day ATR and a trailing stop at one times the 20-day ATR. Your position size may or may not be indicated by the system but will need to stay within your account-based risk control such that the initial stop loss doesn't exceed your Maximum Allowable Risk per trade. The system will then tell you when, if, and how to manually adjust the stop loss, or even add to a position (scaling in), or its opposite (scaling out). It will also clearly tell you under what conditions to manually exit the trade, assuming you have not been stopped out automatically.

That's it. It removes all executive (decision making) capacity from you, the trader, and places that function firmly within the system. It prevents you from losing more than you already decided you could lose in a single trade or collectively, thanks to your risk control. It also prevents you from closing trades out early, which would result in less profits than you could have made. The key thing is that it bypasses your emotions. That, in turn, will make you a consistent trader. It doesn't matter if it makes you a consistently **losing** trader. That can be fixed. The important thing is that it avoids the possibility of suffering a catastrophic loss. One that might end your trading career or, at the very least, take you years to recover from its consequences.

There is not a single successful trader that I know of, and I know way too many, who does not have a trading system (or several) that they follow religiously. Don't try to Dunning-Kruger this.

BOOK FIVE – GENERAL BUSINESS RULES

Rule #19

Don't Reinvent the Wheel

Over the years, I've had people approach me with their grandiose plans to invent the ultimate trading system, the one that never loses. A few times, I've even had people tell me they've created it. Many of these last are scammers, of course, not realizing that I've been around the block way too many times to fall for fairy tales. But enough of them truly think they've discovered that most elusive of unicorns, the system that never loses.

What they'll do is come up with something, and then backtest it like there's no tomorrow, no pun intended. I dislike backtesting almost as much as I dislike demo trading. Everyone's a millionaire backtesting or demo trading. You can massage the past, and make it do anything, just like any decent preacher can support any position with a standard Bible, but you can never trade the past. The only valid test for a system is to trade it, with cold, hard cash.

Now, I'm not saying that you can't come up with a new system. People have. The new system will never be a 100% winner, but you can come up with something new that gives you an edge. Every system out there, after all, was invented by someone at some point in time. But you, you specifically, are very unlikely to come up with one. I'm assuming you are not a well-established trader with a couple of decades' experience under your belt or, let's face it, you wouldn't be reading this book. You don't just start trading or take a course, and suddenly come up with a new system. Yet most beginners somehow think they can, and many choose that as their hill to die on.

I have seen people waste years backtesting and never trading because they're just "this close" to perfecting their infallible system. Don't fall down that rabbit-hole. If you're going to waste years of your life backtesting and demo trading, pick something more fulfilling, like stamp collecting. Of course, I discourage any of my students, as well as people who approach me, from pursuing such a pointless task. Especially when not only has the wheel already been invented, but we have so many wheels to choose from.

There are dozens of systems that work perfectly fine under some very common market conditions. You master a few of these, and you're set. No, they won't give you winners 100% of the time, no system does that, no system ever will do that, but they give you enough of an edge where you can make decent returns year after year after year.

What to Do Instead

Don't waste your time reinventing the wheel. Just use any of the many wheels available to you. This will certainly involve reading more than this book. Also, avoid anyone selling such a system, these systems are usually in the public domain.

I have seen some very sleazy but creative forex outfits selling one of the oldest systems out there as if they had invented it, to the tune of US$1,000 a pop, and I'm told it sold wonderfully. They simply called it something else. When one of my former students started telling me about this wonderful system he'd just bought, and describing it to me, I said, "Boy, that sure sounds a lot like the Ichimoku". I then proceeded to explain that system and showed him some charts using it. He let out an expletive. He tried getting his money back, and last I heard, he was still trying.

The Ichimoku Kinko No Hyo, to give it its full name, was published in the 1960s. Anyone can use it, freely. And I've yet to see a charting system that doesn't come with it standard. Well, except for the charting system this one company was peddling, where you had to pay an extra US$1,000, on top of the US$2,000 or more they charged for the base system, to get the Ichimoku. Under a different name, obviously. Plus, who pays for charting? Metatrader[21] is free and does everything you need and then some.

Which segues nicely into our next rule.

---

[21] https://www.metatrader4.com/en

Rule #20

Don't Pay for Stuff that's Free or Unnecessary

You've all seen what a trader's setup is supposed to look like, right? A massive computer, 3+ screens on top of a very stylish desk, a Bloomberg terminal somewhere close, and the walls in a very tasteful yet subdued color. It's something we've seen hundreds of times in movies, advertisements, and probably in our dreams.

What if I told you that you could do 99% of what I do as a successful trader just using your smartphone? I'm not kidding. Yet, when I started out, I did buy the supercomputer with the 3 screens, and a bunch of professional grade trading software that I had to pay for monthly. That's on top of special software so I could remote into my trading rig from anywhere, and a bunch of other tools I felt were indispensable.

What to Do Instead

Here's what I really needed, and nothing more. It's also what you will need.

- A computer - Any computer that runs any relatively recent version of Windows. Doesn't need to have a huge drive nor massive amounts of memory. It can even be a laptop.
- One screen - You don't need to look at more than one chart at a time, 99% of the time. And when you do, you either place them mosaic style on the one screen, or you flip back and forth between them. Is it more convenient in those rare cases to have multiple screens? Sure, but it's not worth the extra hassle. If you really want to, knock yourself out, but it's overkill. You will also need a much more powerful and expensive computer for such a setup, so the costs pile up quickly.
- An Internet connection - Choose a good provider, not for speed but for reliability. And have some form of backup. A data plan on your smart phone is more than enough. Any alternative way to get online in case your Internet Provider is down.
- Metatrader 4 or 5 - This is all the charting software you will ever need. The version you use, 4 or 5, will depend on what version your broker uses. You will find scores of paid charting systems out there, and they cost thousands of dollars per year. Even if they cost $10, they wouldn't be worth it. I have yet to see a single valuable feature in one of these paid systems that isn't already available on Metatrader[22] or easily added to it.

- A smartphone - I use an iPhone, but there's no reason why you can't use Android. Metatrader has apps for both, which is very convenient when you're not in front of your PC.
- A desk - If you must. There's no reason not to. I simply use a table when necessary, and more often, I just sit in my recliner chair and take advantage of the fact that laptops, as their name indicates, fit in your lap.
- A VPS (Virtual Private Server) - This is optional, but highly recommended. There are many cases when you want your Metatrader to be running 24/7. Especially true if you are copytrading[23]
- An RDP (Remote Desktop Protocol) client/app - Both for your main PC and for your smart phone, especially if you're using a VPS. The RDP client allows you to connect to any other PC or Server that's also connected to the Internet. They are free. No need to pay for any additional licenses of any kind. In fact, RDP comes pre-loaded on any Windows machine.

That's it. Anything else anyone tries to sell you is unnecessary or redundant. Your only other expenses should be books and training, as necessary.

---

[22] https://www.metatrader4.com/en

[23] https://specialfxacademy.com/services/fxcopytrader

Rule #21

Slow and Steady Wins the Race

You know how supermarkets make money? They buy stuff wholesale and sell it retail to millions of customers. Some people go into a supermarket to buy only a single gallon of milk. What's the supermarket's profit on that? Surely less than a dollar. That profit probably doesn't even cover the cashier's time, the electricity used in checking them out, and the 2 plastic bags, because you know that gallon needs to be double bagged. However, many people do buy more than a gallon of milk. And even if milk was all they sold, less than a dollar times millions of gallons every single day is still millions of dollars in profit.

Walmart doesn't expect one guy to walk in one day and buy all their milk, giving them a huge chunk of profit in one go. And neither should you. Not that you're selling milk, but I've pivoted to trades.

You cannot expect one single trade, much less many single trades, to suddenly give you record-breaking profits. That's not the way it works. Instead, you should focus on following your system(s) of choice, taking as many trades as possible. If they collectively add 1% a week to your account, or 5% a month, or 75% a year, or more, that's great. That is all you need. You've heard of death by a thousand cuts? Where no single cut kills you, but collectively, from all of them, you bleed to death? This is the same, but in reverse. No individual trade is going to make you rich, but collectively, all the hundreds or thousands of trades in a year? They are going to make you rich, slowly, but steadily.

And guess what? Every now and then, just because you're showing up every day and following a system, you will get that one amazing trade that may add 10%, 20%, or even more, in one fell swoop. You can't plan for those trades, you can't be expecting them, but they will happen. Take them as a bonus for following the process.

Trading is a long game; it is one of patience. I repeat this a lot because it is one of the common points of failure for traders. They can't afford to take their time, not realizing that that is the only way. There is no quick in the markets, except through luck. Luck doesn't do command performances.

What to Do

I have a very good friend whom I have known for over 40 years. I have invited him to do business with me multiple times over those years, and he has also offered me partnership in his ventures. We've both politely but firmly refused each invitation. We love each other like brothers, but we would never work out as business partners. We have fundamentally opposed philosophies. My friend has been looking for a big score since he started out. He dreams of creating the next Microsoft or finding the next Bitcoin when it's still worth only 13¢. He feels he needs US$100,000,000 to support himself through old age and leave enough for his kids to have a decent lifestyle. Meanwhile, I'm not looking for millions. I'm just looking for more money coming in each month and each year than I can possibly spend, living the way I want to live. I wouldn't know what to do with "millions", but I know exactly what to do with the "thousands" that I already have coming in.

While he's been searching for his big score, I've been living the life, buying properties all cash with the extra money that I can't spend even if I tried, and making other investments. I am worth millions today, from a net worth perspective, without even trying. I accumulated all that over decades, a penny at a time, then a dollar at a time, and so on, until it became thousands at a time. But it didn't start with thousands at a time. And had I tried to force it to be thousands at a time, forget about millions, I'd still be like my dear friend, looking for enough paid work while in his fifties to keep up with the bills and with the Joneses.

I've tried to explain it, but it doesn't get through to him. I verbatim told him just last week, when he offered me a partnership again, that he was chasing US$100,000,000 in one go while ignoring the 100,000,000,000¢ right in front of him. That that many pennies add up to an actual billion dollars, even if they must be picked up one at a time. He still didn't get it. He's not going to get it. And being in his fifties, the likelihood of him lucking into a big score is looking less and less possible by the day.

What **you** should do is go for many, many small constant wins instead of one big one. A million small winning trades are easier to accomplish than one outrageously huge win. As a bonus, while making all the smaller wins, you can still be the recipient of a huge win. Whereas, if you're only chasing the big one, you will ignore the easier, steadier, and much more frequent smaller wins.

Rule #22

Leverage is Necessary

"Give me a lever long enough and a fulcrum on which to place it, and I shall move the world." - Archimedes

Leverage is the ability that your broker provides that enables you to trade as if you had far more money than you have in your account. It's as magical a thing as compound interest. It lets you play in the big leagues. It multiplies your profits, when you're right, but it can wipe you out if you're wrong and misuse it. You can't choose not to use it, but you can learn how to use it, and it all goes back to Risk Control, a topic I often return to.

So. Leverage. You will see leverage expressed as a ratio, for example, 50:1. You may also see it expressed as the margin required to open a certain sized position. Both are saying the same thing, just in different ways.

In the Forex Market, a full lot position is the equivalent of US$100,000 in whatever currency. A minilot is a tenth of that, a US$10,000 position. And a microlot is a tenth of a minilot, a US$1,000 position. You may even find brokers allowing you to trade nanolots, the equivalent of a US$100 position.

A 50:1 leverage means that you need a fiftieth of the position size to open a trade and keep it open. At 50:1 leverage, I would need US$2,000 in my account to keep a full lot position open (US$100,000 divided by 50). The US$2,000 required in this example is called the minimum margin requirement (MMR). As I said above, it's simply two ways of saying the same thing. The leverage multiplies the strength of your US$2,000 fifty-fold, just like a lever multiplies your physical strength.

You will, of course, find different leverage offered on different currency pairs, with 50:1, 33:1, and 20:1 being the most common. It is up to you to determine how much MMR you need to keep your positions open (your broker will have a page with the different leverages or MMR per currency pair), making sure you stay above the MMR. Personally, I never use up more than half the money in my account as margin, since temporary market moves against my position will reduce my account value (same thing as margin) while they play out.

If I used all my money as MMR, and my open positions moved against me by even a penny, I would be under a margin call. That's the term used by brokers to indicate that there isn't enough money in the account to satisfy the minimum margin requirements. Once that happens, you will either be asked to add more money to the account, or the broker will unilaterally close out some or all of your positions.

Why not simply refuse to use leverage and trade only with the money in your account? The same reason we don't attempt to move a boulder by brute strength alone, but instead use a lever. You might be able to move the boulder without a lever, but it would take a lot more time and effort, and you might end up dead, injured, or with the boulder unmoved.

If you trade a full lot with your US$2,000 margin and the currency pair's price moves in your favor by half a cent (50 pips) you would have a profit of US$500 (at $10 a pip). If you traded without leverage, just with your US$2,000 (a 2 minilot position), that same price move in your favor would result in a profit of US$10. That's the power of leverage. Of course, if you had US$100,000 in your account, traded the full lot, and didn't use leverage, you'd have the same US$500 profit. But do you have US$100,000 to trade with? Kudos to you if you do. Whereas many people do have US$2,000. Besides, with leverage, that's a 25% profit on your US$2,000. Without leverage, it's a 0.5% profit on your US$100,000.

Remember, though, that sword cuts both ways. You could lose US$500 just as easily. But we already know we can both win and lose when trading, that we need to control risk, and that playing the odds properly moves those odds in our favor.

What to Do

Do not be afraid of leverage. Do respect it, though, and use it properly, as a multiplier of your account's strength. Also, under normal conditions, even though it is technically borrowed money, only your funds are at risk. Remember, the broker will shut you down well before you lose all **your** money and won't allow you to get anywhere near losing any of **their** money.

Afterword

Remember the main goal always, and that is to never suffer a catastrophic loss. The definition of catastrophic loss is any situation where you lose the capacity to continue trading. If you remain in the game, you can win the game. The rules in this book and the ancillary material are designed to guarantee that you never suffer a catastrophic loss.

Every single failed trader I have met, or you will ever meet, can blame their failure on not following one or more of the rules in this book. Every successful trader I have ever met, or you will ever meet, knows and follows every single rule in this book, consciously or unconsciously.

Should you have a rule you think is important but isn't in this book, please reach out and let me know. If I agree and add it, I will happily share credit with you. This book is not meant to be the final word, it should instead be seen as the beginning of a conversation, and I appreciate anybody who adds to it.

Appendix I

Systems for Trading

I mentioned throughout many of the rules that for you to succeed at trading, you MUST use a system that identifies trades. The proper system will highlight when to enter trades, at what risk level, when to adjust them, and when to exit them. This is critical. Just like serious companies do not make a move without engaging in market analysis, product testing, product placement, and a dozen other activities before even thinking of manufacturing a product, so too must you treat every trade with absolute sobriety.

Systems are what allow you to do this. In my first book, whose emphasis was on the basics and keeping things simple, I focused on things that anyone should be able to master in days, if not hours, and would allow them to start showing a profit while keeping risk under control. I could have introduced more complex systems, but I deliberately chose not to. The reason is that traders need to learn how to walk before they can learn how to run. Traders who try to start at the more complex end of things almost invariably fail. I wanted to give people a better chance at succeeding.

If, for some reason, you arrived at this book before reading my first book, Making it in the Forex Market[24], I strongly urge you to pause here, go back, read that book, master its contents, and only then proceed with the following

---

[24] http://amzn.to/3ANrLF5

material. You cannot and should not put the cart before the horse. Trading is one of the least forgiving activities you will ever engage in, one where even the professionals can self-destruct. Doing it the right way, following an orderly path, makes it far more likely that you will be on the winners' podium when all the dust settles.

One of the most difficult things I have faced as a trading teacher and mentor, is convincing my students that the basics, plus my rules, plus the use of a system or systems, are the **only** way to achieve lasting success trading the market. There are an infinite number of ways to fail. Every failing trader seems to come up with his or her own variation. But there is only one way to succeed permanently, and this is it.

Now, there are many systems. The important thing is to follow one and follow it to the letter. If you want to follow more than one system at a time, you can, but you must do so on separate accounts. You cannot commingle systems. Also, not all systems are good. I will eventually publish my personal catalog of systems that I know for a fact work. Even those, however, will not all work all of the time, and a savvy trader must know when to use a system, when not to, and have the patience to wait for the right time. The beauty is that at any one time, whatever the market conditions are, you'll find a system that is well suited for it. That doesn't mean you should trade in all market conditions, but it does mean that you could, if you're comfortable in all market conditions.

I tend to stay out of trendless or sideways market, two terms for the same thing. This is when the market is trading sideways in a very narrow range, not moving up or down, for an extended period. It's just not worth my while. That doesn't mean it can't be traded successfully. It can. But it takes a lot more work for very little profit. I stay out until a new trend establishes itself. I know many traders who will trade in such a market, and make smaller but frequent profits from it. Each to his own. And, yes, there are systems for that.

My personal forte are longer term systems, though, those referred to as "position trading" in Rule #10. I consider these the safest and most profitable. New traders often have the urge to be constantly trading. They think that they must always be in the market. This is a myth. Some very successful traders take only a handful of trades a year, and they make a tidy living from those few trades. One of my accounts sees around 30 trades a year. It usually does better than 100% yearly returns. Another sees 200 or so trades a year and comes in at around 75% returns a year. These are average annualized returns over more than 10 years, so it's not the same returns every single year, but they average out to that. Both make money consistently, and both suit my temperament. I also spread out the risk by trading two different systems.

Now we've fully introduced the subject, let's look at my systems. Which, for the record, are mine in the sense that I use them, not in the sense that I created them. This is another rule, Rule #19, Don't Reinvent the Wheel.

Turtle Trading

Back in the eighties, two very successful traders made a bet. One of them, Richard Dennis, said that he could raise traders like people in Singapore raised turtles. That's why the system is known as Turtle Trading. The other trader, William Eckhardt, disagreed. For the full story, variations on the system, and documented results, please read Michael Covel's brilliant book on the subject, The Complete Turtle Trader.[25]

Now, you read before that I was disabused early into my teaching career of the notion that anyone can become a trader. I stand by that. And Dennis seems to have felt similarly. He devised a rather long and seemingly nonsensical questionnaire that he used to weed out the majority of applicants who came in after he posted an ad in the newspaper. He specifically seems to have rejected anyone with prior trading experience. He wanted blank slates who would follow simple instructions to the letter.

Dennis's "Turtles" were given very brief training, a set of rules (the system), and money to trade with. Anyone breaking any of the rules was promptly dismissed. Those who stayed the course went on to become some of the most legendary traders of the eighties, nineties, and beyond. Needless to say, Dennis won the bet. I use the system he

---

[25] https://amzn.to/3TcYbQV

gave his "Turtles", with no variation, to this day. It is responsible for the bulk of my trading profit every year. Here is the system Dennis called, System One.

Instrument being traded: Any currency pair that is within your tradable pairs.
Chart View/Timeframe: A daily chart or even a table with daily closing price. Note that this system is only to be used with daily price action, no other timeframe.
Entry Signal: A four-week (20 candle) price breakout. If price makes a new four-week high or low, a trade is entered in the direction of the breakout. A new high indicates a buy, and a new low indicates a sell.
Stop loss: Twice the 20-day ATR (Average True Range). This is an indicator available in all charting systems that tells you how many pips a pair is moving, on average, every day. If the ATR is 75 pips, for example, then the initial stop loss will be set at 150 pips.
Exit Signal: A long (buy) trade will be exited when the pair makes a breakout two-week (10 candle) low. A short (sell) trade will be exited when the pair makes a breakout two-week (10 candle) high.
Filters: If the immediately previous signal on the chart was a winner, irrespective of whether that signal was taken, the new signal will be ignored. This prevents entries in choppy as well as sideways markets. However, if the previous signal was or would have been a losing trade, then the new signal should be taken. The direction of the previous signal is

irrelevant. That is, it doesn't have to be in the same direction as the new signal.

That's it. Simple, and with no opportunity for confusion. It takes about 5 to 10 minutes a day to scan all your charts and clearly see whether there is a signal to enter a trade or to close an existing one. This is clearly a position trading system, and you can expect to be in a trade for weeks, if not months, when it's a profitable trade. Do people fail and/or lose money with this system? Absolutely Not every trade will be a winner, of course, nor will every pair be suitable for it. You will learn which are which as you use it, and I can't tell you because the pairs that work brilliantly with it this year might not be the best next year. Markets change over time, in cycles. But the most common reason for failure using this or any other system, is the trader's inability to follow the system.

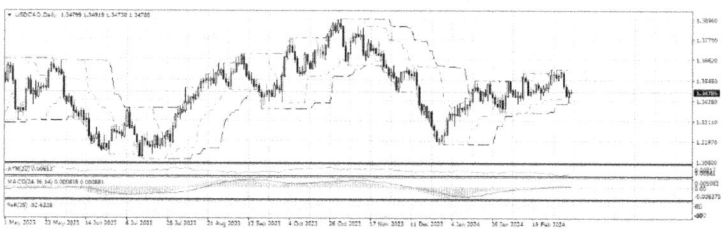

Figure 2 - Turtle Trading System One Indicator

I have set up a custom indicator in my charts which draws these Turtle lines for easy monitoring. I'll be happy to send the indicator by email to anyone interested. It will work on Metatrader 4 or 5. The black dashed lines are the four-week highs and lows, and the red dashed lines are the two-week highs and lows. It is crystal clear when price crosses a line.

3-Screen System

I first encountered this system in Dr. Alexander Elder's excellent book, Trading for a Living. While looking it up, I noticed he's put out a new edition, The New Trading for a Living.[26] I started using it due to its simplicity and straightforwardness. I quickly discovered how useful it was for swing trading. It keeps me busy in between signals from the Turtle System described above and adds nicely to my bottom line.

Without further ado, here is the 3-Screen System.

Instrument being traded: Any currency pair that is within your tradable pairs.
Chart View 1: A weekly chart, which we will call the first screen. The key thing here will not be the candles themselves, but rather a trend indicator, such as the MACD with its default parameters.
Chart View 2: A daily chart, which we will call the second screen. The key thing here will not be the candles themselves, but rather an oscillator indicator, such as the Force Index, with a period of 2, and set to exponential. The idea being to catch deviations from the weekly trend. Don't worry if you don't understand any of that. It is visual and easily understood on a chart.

---

[26] https://amzn.to/4a678ST

Filters, Entry Signals, and Stop Loss: On an upslope in the weekly chart's MACD, which means that the current bar is higher than the previous bar in the histogram, we look to buy. If it is a downslope, we look to sell. So immediately on looking at a weekly chart (first screen) we know whether we are wanting to buy (upslope), sell (downslope), or stay out (flat). Note that we aren't doing anything yet, but we've already eliminated one direction, or even both. On the daily chart of the same pair, the Force line will either be below the centerline or above it. We are looking for divergence here. If the weekly told us to buy, we want the Force line to be below the center line. If it is, we set a buy stop order 5 pips above the previous candle's high with a stop loss 5 pips below that same candle's low. If the weekly told us to sell, we want the Force line to be above the center line. If it is, we set a sell stop order 5 pips below the previous candle's low with a stop loss 5 pips above that same candle's high. Any other condition is a no go, and we move to the next pair. The pending order becomes the third screen, hence the system's name. Not because there is an actual screen to look at, but because we are screening out (eliminating) trades at each step.

Exit Signal: Set a trailing stop at half the distance between the previous candle's high and low.

That's it. A but more complicated in words, but quite simple visually. You can check these charts once a day. This is clearly a swing trading system, and you can expect to be in a trade anywhere between hours and a few days, when it's a profitable trade. Do people fail and/or lose money with this system? This one has the same caveats as the prior system, and any system, for that matter. Not every trade will be a winner, nor will every pair be suitable for it. You will learn which are which as you use it, and I can't tell you because the pairs that work brilliantly with it this month might not be the best next month. Markets change over time, in cycles. But the most common reason for failure using this or any other system, is the trader's inability to follow the system.

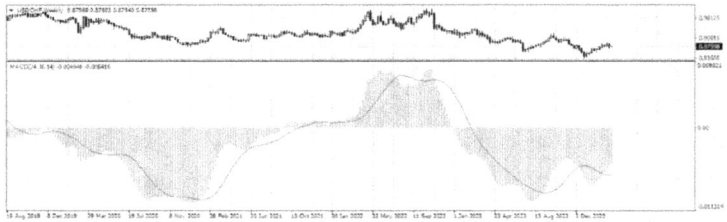
Figure 3 - Weekly Chart of USDCHF with MACD Histogram

The MACD Histogram is on the bottom of this weekly chart, and I make it large so I can easily see the slope. In this case, you can clearly see that it is going up, hence I am looking for a buy signal.

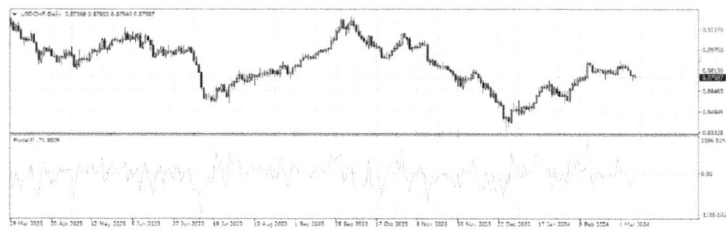
Figure 4 - Daily Chart of USDCHF with Force Index

The Force Index is on the bottom of this daily chart, also enlarged, and the line is below the center line, confirming the buy. I would then set a buy stop pending order 5 pips above yesterday's candle, with a stop loss 5 pips below that same candle's low. I measured that candle, and discover it is 50 pips from top to bottom, so I set a trailing stop at 25 pips. That's it, I leave it be. If it hasn't triggered by the following day, and the conditions are still valid for an entry, I adjust the entry price, stop, and trailing stop to the next candle. If the conditions no longer indicate a trade, I delete the pending order.

One Last Thing

If you enjoyed this book, please help me spread the word. Tell your friends. Post about it on social media with a link to Amazon and leave an honest review there.

You can also keep track of what we're up to, find updated trading advice, and a lot more advice that just couldn't make it into this book, on our website at:

https://www.specialfxacademy.com/

I enjoy hearing from my readers and from traders. Also reach out to me if you find any mistakes in the content of this book, or if you feel an idea wasn't presented clearly enough. You'll be helping me greatly if you point them out to me. You can always email me directly at:

trader@specialfxacademy.com

If you're interested in mentoring, I offer one on one coaching to get you to the next level of trading in the Forex Market. I do not believe in automated courses, so they are both individual and one on one, and as such I do not take many students on simultaneously. Email me and be patient. Open spots become available as previous students "graduate". The bulk of my day is spent either trading or enjoying the fruits of my labor. But I also believe in paying it forward. I had many kind traders help me out when I was starting, and I also had some very good mentors that I happily paid, for their time.

Do not become one of those people who buy course after course, trading system after trading system, and then complain that they're not making any money. There's no need for that. You only need to be trained once, and you don't need every new system that gets released every week promising to be the Holy Grail. There's no such thing. Just hard work, knowledge, and practice. Anyone making hundreds of thousands of dollars selling courses, as one company I am familiar with does, is probably not trading for a living. And if their people aren't trading, what can they possibly teach you?

I promised my first student ever that I would charge him for my coaching and that alone. If one day I updated what I teach, he'd automatically have access to the updates. If I suddenly start releasing Holy Grail after Holy Grail (which I won't because they don't exist, but if I did), they'd also be included at no additional cost until the day I go on to the Great Forex Market in the Sky, where every trade is always a winner. I extended that same promise to every other student after. No marketing calls every day asking for your credit card in return for the newest shiny object. I promise. Saves me a bunch of money, too, by not having a marketing department.

Even this book, which I will inevitably update as I find typos or other things to adjust. If you bought it on Kindle or any other electronic platform, it will update itself on your device automatically and at no extra cost. When I need money, I'll place a trade. It's as simple as that. So, thanks for coming along on this journey. I hope I have made it an enjoyable and profitable one for you.

ABOUT THE AUTHOR

Andres E. Pedraza has held high level positions at the New York Stock Exchange, Euronext, and Fannie Mae (Federal National Mortgage Association - FNMA), among others. He's overseen state of the art IT operations for multinational corporations, delivering high availability services to trading floors and other mission critical areas, and leading some of the teams that designed, implemented, and operated new IT projects during his tenure at each company. Thanks to his positions at the exchanges, he couldn't help but be exposed to trading, strategies, equity management, portfolio management, and how successful traders create wealth. It was an invaluable education which he hopes to pass on to others who may not have had the fortune to be similarly exposed. Today he is an entrepreneur and a trader.

He can be reached directly at trader@specialfxacademy.com.

www.ingramcontent.com/pod-product-compliance
Lightning Source LLC
Chambersburg PA
CBHW071514220526
45472CB00003B/1018